Gun Control

Other Books of Related Interest

Opposing Viewpoints Series
Government Gridlock
Mass Shootings
Police Reform

At Issue Series
Partisanship
Policing in America
Public Outrage and Protest

Current Controversies Series
Domestic Extremism
Hate Groups
States' Rights and the Role of the Federal Government

> "Congress shall make no law … abridging the freedom of speech, or of the press."
>
> *First Amendment to the U.S. Constitution*

The basic foundation of our democracy is the First Amendment guarantee of freedom of expression. The Opposing Viewpoints series is dedicated to the concept of this basic freedom and the idea that it is more important to practice it than to enshrine it.

OPPOSING VIEWPOINTS® SERIES

| Gun Control

Lisa Idzikowski, Book Editor

LIVINGSTON PUBLIC LIBRARY
10 Robert Harp Drive
Livingston, NJ 07039

Published in 2024 by Greenhaven Publishing, LLC
2544 Clinton Street,
Buffalo NY 14224

Copyright © 2024 by Greenhaven Publishing, LLC

First Edition

All rights reserved. No part of this book may be reproduced in any form
without permission in writing from the publisher, except by a reviewer.

Articles in Greenhaven Publishing anthologies are often edited for length to meet page
requirements. In addition, original titles of these works are changed to clearly present
the main thesis and to explicitly indicate the author's opinion. Every effort is made to
ensure that Greenhaven Publishing accurately reflects the original intent of the authors.
Every effort has been made to trace the owners of the copyrighted material.

Cover image: meeboonstudio/Shutterstock.com

Library of Congress CataloginginPublication Data

Names: Idzikowski, Lisa, editor.
Title: Gun control / edited by Lisa Idzikowski.
Description: First edition. | New York : Greenhaven Publishing, 2024. | Series:
Opposing viewpoints | Includes bibliographical references and index.
Identifiers: ISBN 9781534509559 (pbk.) | ISBN 9781534509566 (library bound)
Subjects: LCSH: Firearms--Law and legislation--United States--Juvenile literature.
| Firearms--Licenses--United States--Juvenile literature. | Gun control--United
States--Juvenile literature. | Firearms ownership--Juvenile literature.
Classification: LCC KF394.G866 2024 | DDC 344.7305'33--dc23

Manufactured in the United States of America

Website: http://greenhavenpublishing.com

Contents

The Importance of Opposing Viewpoints	11
Introduction	14

Chapter 1: Should Guns Be Controlled?

Chapter Preface	18
1. Politics Distorts the Second Amendment and Gun Ownership *Jonathan Parker*	19
2. Firearms Endanger Children and Teens *Marc A. Zimmerman, Dr. Patrick Carter, and Rebecca Cunningham*	25
3. Guns Should Be Controlled for the Sake of Young People *Amy Sherman*	30
4. The Majority of Americans Want Gun Control *Austin Sarat*	34
5. Does Australia Have the Answer for Gun Control? *Rick Sarre*	38
Periodical and Internet Sources Bibliography	42

Chapter 2: How Do Politics Impact Gun Control?

Chapter Preface	45
1. American Citizens, Not Politicians, Are Responsible for the Current State of Gun Control *Jarrett Stepman*	46
2. Democrats and Republicans Agree on Some Points of Gun Legislation *Monika L. McDermott and David R. Jones*	51
3. The NRA Effectively Prevents Meaningful Gun Control Legislation *Thomas Gift*	56

4. Republicans and Gun Owners Favor Armed
   Teachers in Schools   62
   Aimee Dinnin Huff and Michelle Barnhart
5. Facts, Opinions, and Beliefs About Guns in America   67
   Katherine Schaeffer
6. In Some States, Gun Laws Are Weakened After
   Mass Shooting Incidents   73
   Christopher Poliquin
7. Will New Gun Laws Stem Gun Violence?   77
   Pew Research Center

Periodical and Internet Sources Bibliography   84

Chapter 3: Is Gun Control Economically Feasible?

Chapter Preface   87
1. Gun Lobby Money Prevents Meaningful Gun Control   88
   Joseph Stepansky
2. More Guns Equals More Money for Gunmakers
   and More Gun Violence   93
   Michael Siegel
3. Do Gun Buyback Programs Work to Reduce
   Gun Deaths?   97
   David Bright
4. Can Gun Makers Be Held Responsible for
   Their Products?   104
   Allen Rostron
5. The Social Consequences of Mass Gun Violence   110
   Arash Javanbakht

Periodical and Internet Sources Bibliography   117

Chapter 4: Will Gun Control Be Possible in the Future?

Chapter Preface   120

1. Americans Are Worried About Potential
   Gun Violence   121
   The University of Chicago
2. Lax Gun Laws Are Fueling Gun Violence,
   and It Must Stop   126
   Michael Lyle
3. Gun Laws Must Be Strengthened   130
   Guy Lamb
4. Following the Examples of Other Nations Can
   Help Tackle Gun Violence   137
   Jonathan Masters
5. The United States Needs to Emulate Other
   Developed Nations in Gun Control   145
   John Donohue
6. Federal Funding for Firearms Research Must
   Expand to Stem Gun Violence   153
   Kirsten Weir

Periodical and Internet Sources Bibliography   160

For Further Discussion   162
Organizations to Contact   164
Bibliography of Books   168
Index   170

The Importance of Opposing Viewpoints

Perhaps every generation experiences a period in time in which the populace seems especially polarized, starkly divided on the important issues of the day and gravitating toward the far ends of the political spectrum and away from a consensus-facilitating middle ground. The world that today's students are growing up in and that they will soon enter into as active and engaged citizens is deeply fragmented in just this way. Issues relating to terrorism, immigration, women's rights, minority rights, race relations, health care, taxation, wealth and poverty, the environment, policing, military intervention, the proper role of government—in some ways, perennial issues that are freshly and uniquely urgent and vital with each new generation—are currently roiling the world.

If we are to foster a knowledgeable, responsible, active, and engaged citizenry among today's youth, we must provide them with the intellectual, interpretive, and critical-thinking tools and experience necessary to make sense of the world around them and of the all-important debates and arguments that inform it. After all, the outcome of these debates will in large measure determine the future course, prospects, and outcomes of the world and its peoples, particularly its youth. If they are to become successful members of society and productive and informed citizens, students need to learn how to evaluate the strengths and weaknesses of someone else's arguments, how to sift fact from opinion and fallacy, and how to test the relative merits and validity of their own opinions against the known facts and the best possible available information. The landmark series Opposing Viewpoints has been providing students with just such critical-thinking skills and exposure to the debates surrounding society's most urgent contemporary issues for many years, and it continues to serve this essential role with undiminished commitment, care, and rigor.

The key to the series's success in achieving its goal of sharpening students' critical-thinking and analytic skills resides in its title—

Opposing Viewpoints. In every intriguing, compelling, and engaging volume of this series, readers are presented with the widest possible spectrum of distinct viewpoints, expert opinions, and informed argumentation and commentary, supplied by some of today's leading academics, thinkers, analysts, politicians, policy makers, economists, activists, change agents, and advocates. Every opinion and argument anthologized here is presented objectively and accorded respect. There is no editorializing in any introductory text or in the arrangement and order of the pieces. No piece is included as a "straw man," an easy ideological target for cheap point-scoring. As wide and inclusive a range of viewpoints as possible is offered, with no privileging of one particular political ideology or cultural perspective over another. It is left to each individual reader to evaluate the relative merits of each argument—as he or she sees it, and with the use of ever-growing critical-thinking skills—and grapple with his or her own assumptions, beliefs, and perspectives to determine how convincing or successful any given argument is and how the reader's own stance on the issue may be modified or altered in response to it.

This process is facilitated and supported by volume, chapter, and selection introductions that provide readers with the essential context they need to begin engaging with the spotlighted issues, with the debates surrounding them, and with their own perhaps shifting or nascent opinions on them. In addition, guided reading and discussion questions encourage readers to determine the authors' point of view and purpose, interrogate and analyze the various arguments and their rhetoric and structure, evaluate the arguments' strengths and weaknesses, test their claims against available facts and evidence, judge the validity of the reasoning, and bring into clearer, sharper focus the reader's own beliefs and conclusions and how they may differ from or align with those in the collection or those of their classmates.

Research has shown that reading comprehension skills improve dramatically when students are provided with compelling, intriguing, and relevant "discussable" texts. The subject matter of these collections could not be more compelling, intriguing, or urgently relevant to today's students and the world they are poised to inherit. The anthologized articles and the reading and discussion questions that are included with them also provide the basis for stimulating, lively, and passionate classroom debates. Students who are compelled to anticipate objections to their own argument and identify the flaws in those of an opponent read more carefully, think more critically, and steep themselves in relevant context, facts, and information more thoroughly. In short, using discussable text of the kind provided by every single volume in the Opposing Viewpoints series encourages close reading, facilitates reading comprehension, fosters research, strengthens critical thinking, and greatly enlivens and energizes classroom discussion and participation. The entire learning process is deepened, extended, and strengthened.

For all of these reasons, Opposing Viewpoints continues to be exactly the right resource at exactly the right time—when we most need to provide readers with the critical-thinking tools and skills that will not only serve them well in school but also in their careers and their daily lives as decision-making family members, community members, and citizens. This series encourages respectful engagement with and analysis of opposing viewpoints and fosters a resulting increase in the strength and rigor of one's own opinions and stances. As such, it helps make readers "future ready," and that readiness will pay rich dividends for the readers themselves, for the citizenry, for our society, and for the world at large.

Introduction

> "When we compare the states head-to-head on the top 50 gun safety policies, a clear pattern emerges. States with strong laws see less gun violence. Indeed, the 14 states that have failed to put basic protections into place—'national failures' on our scale—have nearly triple the rate of gun deaths as the eight national gun safety leaders."
>
> —*Everytown for Gun Safety 2023*

Firearms and their use as weapons are nothing new. From 1364, the year of the first recorded firearm use, through the years of the Winchester rifle, "the gun that won the West," to 1892 when the first automatic handguns were produced, firearms have been a part of civilization. It is noteworthy to wonder if or when during this time period people began to worry about controlling guns or gun violence.

As defined by *Merriam-Webster*, the phrase "gun control" was first used in 1964 to mean the "regulation of the selling, owning, and use of guns."[1] The National Rifle Association (NRA) has a different take on the term gun control and defines it as the "laws and ordinances that restrict how law-abiding citizens can buy, own, or use firearms," and these ordinances vary at state and local levels.[2]

To state it mildly, gun control is a hotly debated topic in the United States. Its opponents and proponents argue vigorously and often persist in defending their convictions without compromise.

Interestingly, a large portion—but not all—of the bickering and protesting falls neatly along a partisan divide, with Republicans typically being against strong gun control and Democrats favoring it. A June 2023 survey conducted by Pew Research Center points to several key ideas surrounding the gun control debate. Pew found that about four-in-ten adults in the United States live in a gun-owning household.[3] In those households, Republicans and right-leaning independents are more than two times as likely to personally own a gun, and almost three-quarters of gun owners say they have firearms because they feel better protected that way.

According to Gallup, 63 percent of Americans are dissatisfied with U.S. gun laws (based on a survey done in January 2023).[4] So why does there seem to be a stalemate over gun control in the United States? Other countries have made significant inroads into this problem, and statistically reduced gun deaths by a number of laws and restrictions on firearms. Gun control is a complex issue, but besides the partisan divide a couple other reasons stand out as impediments to meaningful gun control.

One is economics. There is simply a lot of money being made by gun manufacturers and the people they employ. Another economic factor is that the U.S. gun lobby financially supports elected officials that support their cause. Yet another frequently cited reason put up against any form of gun control is the Second Amendment of the United States Constitution. Gun control opponents argue that this amendment clearly upholds the right of any American citizen to bear arms without limits. Of course, gun control proponents do not agree on this interpretation of the law. Some believe that the sheer number of guns being held by people increases gun violence.

Clearly, gun control is a divisive issue in the United States. Even with six-in-ten U.S. adults saying that they see gun violence as a major problem, can anything be done? Experts have many ideas on how to combat firearm violence in the future. Funding for gun control research based on scientific data, improving community and social services, emulating the gun control policies of other successful countries, and other ideas outlined in the viewpoints

Gun Control

in this volume explore the practical factors of gun control as well as differing perspectives on its relationship to individual rights.

This timely debate surrounding the issue of gun control is explored in *Opposing Viewpoints: Gun Control*, shedding light on this divisive and ongoing contemporary issue.

Notes

1. "Gun Control," Merriam-Webster, https://www.merriam-webster.com/dictionary/gun%20control.
2. "Why Gun Control Doesn't Work," National Rifle Association Institute for Legislative Action, https://www.nraila.org/why-gun-control-doesn-t-work/.
3. Katherine Schaeffer, "Key Facts About Americans and Guns," Pew Research Center, September 13, 2023, https://www.pewresearch.org/short-reads/2023/09/13/key-facts-about-americans-and-guns/.
4. Megan Brenan, "Dissatisfaction with U.S. Gun Laws Hits New High," Gallup, February 15, 2023, https://news.gallup.com/poll/470588/dissatisfaction-gun-laws-hits-new-high.aspx.

CHAPTER 1

| Should Guns Be Controlled?

Chapter Preface

Should guns be controlled? Should U.S. adults have the right to own a gun? These may be some of the most hotly debated issues in the United States today. Interestingly, according to the Pew Research Center, in a survey conducted in June of 2023, four-in-ten adults said that they lived in a household with a gun, and that three-in-ten of them personally owned a firearm. Almost three-quarters of these gun owners cite personal protection as the reason for gun ownership, with other reasons being hunting, sport shooting, gun collecting, and the use of guns for a job. All these reasons for gun ownership display a wide appreciation of firearms.

This controversial issue appears in news media regularly, whether it's a protest over conceal and carry laws, reports of the latest mass shooting incident, a school board wanting its teachers to be armed, or a gun rally hosted by the National Rifle Association (NRA). Tempers often run high, and opinions about gun control seem to generally follow along political party lines and affiliations.

Viewpoints in this chapter analyze the gun control issue in a variety of ways. Several of the viewpoints take a look at the U.S. Constitution's Second Amendment and how people use the amendment to argue for or against gun ownership. Other viewpoints provide information about the effect of gun violence on young people in the United States, or how politicians and lobbyists seem to be acting in direct opposition to a majority of U.S. voters wanting gun control laws. Finally, readers get a look at gun control in Australia and New Zealand and how these countries are effectively decreasing gun violence.

Viewpoint 1

> "The Amendment is a telling reminder of America's longstanding relationship with guns that goes back to its colonial heritage and has developed a strong and popular mythology surrounding this legacy. But it is not a clear endorsement of the right to own a gun."

Politics Distorts the Second Amendment and Gun Ownership

Jonathan Parker

In the following viewpoint, Jonathan Parker dissects the issue of Second Amendment gun ownership rights and how they intersect with gun control and are interpreted by pro-gun ownership supporters. Parker contends that the Second Amendment has played no part in gun ownership laws or legal battles until fairly recently. He maintains that politics is playing an outsized part in this debate and continues to distort the actual data of crime statistics which fuels gun ownership. Jonathan Parker is a senior lecturer in politics at Keele University in the UK. He conducts research and writes on educational policy and politics.

"Explainer: what is the 2nd Amendment and how does it impact US gun control?," by Jonathan Parker, The Conversation, June 15, 2016. https://theconversation.com/explainer-what-is-the-2nd-amendment-and-how-does-it-impact-us-gun-control-61068. Licensed under CC-BY ND 4.0 International.

As you read, consider the following questions:

1. As stated in the viewpoint, does the Second Amendment endorse the right to own a gun?
2. Why do gun owners tend to own firearms, according to Parker?
3. According to the data cited in this viewpoint, are guns becoming more or less available?

The Second Amendment to the Constitution is a touchstone for the many people who identify with American society's enduring affinity for firearms. And every time there is an atrocity, such as the mass shooting in Orlando, debate inevitably settles on how this part of the Constitution effectively prevents the adoption of workable gun control measures.

But ironically, the Amendment played almost no substantial part in legal or constitutional jurisprudence involving gun ownership until 2008 and even the recent change in Supreme Court interpretations does not give it a significant role in gun regulation. The importance of the Second Amendment lies much more in its symbolism for those people defending gun ownership and as a rallying point for those supporters.

The Amendment is a telling reminder of America's longstanding relationship with guns that goes back to its colonial heritage and has developed a strong and popular mythology surrounding this legacy. But it is not a clear endorsement of the right to own a gun. The text reads:

> A well regulated Militia, being necessary to the security of a free State, the right of the people to keep and bear Arms, shall not be infringed.

The Amendment came out of the colonies' longstanding suspicion of standing armies, accentuated by the recent War of Independence against Great Britain. It sought to enshrine protections for local and state militias, who would provide a bulwark against any possible encroachment of power by the new national government—and its national army—which was established by the Constitution in 1789.

The Second Amendment was always about federalism, protecting the power of the states to have and regulate militias rather than granting individual rights, and the courts interpreted it that way consistently until two cases in 2008 and 2010 completely upended more than two centuries of legal and constitutional history.

Legal Frontiers

In the case of *District of Columbia v. Heller*, 554 U.S. 570 (2008), the Supreme Court held that the Second Amendment protects an individual right to possess a firearm—independent of any service in a militia—for legal purposes such as self-defense. In a subsequent case, *McDonald v. Chicago*, 561 U.S. 3025 (2010), the Court extended this protection against bans by all state and local governments.

These cases established the individual right to gun ownership for the first time—but, significantly, they were only applied in relation to absolute bans. The Supreme Court continues to allow almost all restrictions on firearms short of an outright ban. It is the politics of gun regulation that is much more important if you want to understand the gun debate in the US. The Second Amendment, meanwhile, is a political symbol rather than a strong legal protection.

Declining Ownership and Homicides

An understanding of the place of guns in American culture is needed to fully understand the issue of gun regulation. The General Social Survey (GSS), has found that gun ownership has declined from 49% of households in 1973 to 34% in 2010, though Gallup opinion polls report a lower figure, unchanged from 1972 to 2010 at 43%. Whichever figure is most accurate, a substantial portion of American households own a gun. Traditionally, hunting was the main purpose for gun ownership but it has declined from 49%

in 1999 to 32% in 2013. Personal protection has now become the main reason cited by gun owners, rising from 26% in 1999 to 48% in 2013.

Despite worries over personal safety, fuelled by widespread media coverage of regular mass shootings, the homicide rate from firearms has fallen hugely in the U.S. since the 1990s. Compared with 1993, the peak of U.S. gun homicides, the firearm homicide rate was 49% lower in 2010. The rate for other violent crimes with a firearm was 75% lower in 2011 than in 1993. While violent crime has plummeted since the 1990s, however, mass shootings consume most efforts around gun control today. People believe that crime has gone up rather than down—and this continuing fear of crime influences gun policy.

Opinion Polarised

Public opinion has been decidedly in favor of stricter gun control for decades, but the recent polarization of politics in the U.S. has also influenced people's views on guns. Support for gun control is now roughly matched with support for gun rights in the wider population.

The main areas of gun regulation concern limiting who can purchase a gun. There have been large majorities in favor of restrictions such as background checks for those with criminal records, limiting access for the mentally ill, and creating a national database to track gun sales. Bans on assault rifles, such as the AR-15, used in Orlando are more controversial. These sorts of weapons were banned in 1994 under the Clinton administration but the law was allowed to lapse in 2004 and stands no chance of being re-enacted by the current Congress.

Party Lines

Differing views of gun control across party lines are much more evident now, with Republicans less likely to support a national database or assault weapon ban. These issues have erupted into the presidential campaign. Hillary Clinton called for stronger

Mental Health and Gun Control

Congress is looking to pass a bipartisan gun safety proposal. And if it succeeds, the bill could come with a hefty investment in mental health treatment.

Lawmakers have yet to solidify their plans, but they've said a Senate bill would include bolstering school-based mental health services, crisis intervention, substance use disorder services, and suicide prevention.

Mental health providers say they'll take all the federal resources they can get, but they aren't convinced it will do much to prevent mass shootings.

Dr. Jeff Temple, a psychologist and founding director of the Center for Violence Prevention at the University of Texas Medical Branch, wrote an op-ed originally published in the *Austin American-Statesman:*

Making psychiatric disease the bogeyman is politically expedient—it allows policymakers to shy away from the true culprit. It also fits into how the public often views mental illness—as something to fear. Afterall, what else would cause someone to do something so heinous? The problem with this thinking is that it's wrong.

There's little evidence that people with mental health issues are more likely to assault or kill someone with a gun. In fact, people with mental illnesses are more likely to be the victims of this violence.

One area where mental health and guns do collide is suicide, which accounts for thousands more firearm deaths every year than homicides, according to data from the Centers for Disease Control and Prevention.

What's the nature of the connection between mental health and gun violence? And if it's tenuous, why is it brought up in the wake of tragedy?

"Mental Health, Gun Violence, And Why America Connects Them," National Public Radio Inc. (NPR), June 21, 2022.

background checks and a national database, while Donald Trump—who used to support stricter gun control—accepted the endorsement of the National Rifle Association (NRA) and claimed that Clinton "wants to take away Americans' guns." These statements are largely symbolic as neither party appears eager to engage in a strong attempt to enact gun control due to the potential for a backlash from gun enthusiasts.

The most prominent change in state laws regarding guns in recent times has been to make guns more, rather than less, available. In reaction to the massacre at Sandy Hook Elementary School in 2012, Wayne LaPierre, the NRA vice president, argued that "the only thing that will stop a bad guy with a gun is a good guy with a gun."

States adopted this approach, with 41 adopting laws allowing the carrying of concealed guns by 2014. Debates rage over whether this availability makes the public more or less safe, but it is the sharp edge of the current debate in the states. Meanwhile, in Sandy Hook, Newtown—and now Orlando – hundreds of families continue to mourn their dead as mass shootings continue with a dispiriting regularity.

VIEWPOINT 2

> *"Firearms are the second leading cause of death among U.S. children and adolescents, after car crashes. Firearm deaths occur at a rate over three times higher than drownings."*

Firearms Endanger Children and Teens

Marc A. Zimmerman, Dr. Patrick Carter, and Rebecca Cunningham

In the following viewpoint, Marc A. Zimmerman, Dr. Patrick Carter, and Rebecca Cunningham analyze the issue of firearms and its impact on injury and death among children and adolescents. The authors identify the groups of children and teens that are most negatively affected by firearms. They present statistics surrounding the issue of firearms and injury and differentiate between homicides and suicides. The authors further explain that this phenomenon is a specifically American issue. Marc A. Zimmerman, Dr. Patrick Carter, and Rebecca Cunningham all work in the medical field at the University of Michigan, where Zimmerman is a professor of public health, Carter is an assistant professor of emergency medicine, and Cunningham is a professor of emergency medicine.

"The facts on the US children and teens killed by firearms," by Marc A Zimmerman, Dr. Patrick Carter, and Rebecca Cunningham, The Conversation, August 6, 2019. https://theconversation.com/the-facts-on-the-us-children-and-teens-killed-by-firearms-118318. Licensed under CC-BY-ND 4.0 International.

As you read, consider the following questions:

1. According to the authors, what is the leading cause of death for children and teens in the U.S.?
2. Why does the U.S. stand out with respect to teen firearm deaths, according to the authors?
3. Which group uses research to make firearm ownership safer, as reported in this viewpoint?

Injury is the leading cause of death for U.S. children and adolescents, accounting for over 60% of all deaths in this group.

Many of these deaths occur during fun, everyday activities, like swimming in the backyard pool or during a family car ride. But a disproportionate and disturbing number of these deaths in the U.S. occur as a result of firearms.

Firearms are the second leading cause of death among U.S. children and adolescents, after car crashes. Firearm deaths occur at a rate over three times higher than drownings.

We have dedicated our careers to understanding violence and injury prevention, including how firearm injury and deaths happen and how they can be prevented.

Causes of injury and death due to motor vehicle crashes have steadily declined over the last 20 years, but death and injury due to firearms has remained about the same over the same period.

Firearm Death Rates

Since 2013, fatal firearm injuries for children and teens have risen unabated.

Rates of death from firearms among ages 14 to 17 are now 22.5% higher than motor vehicle-related death rates. In the U.S., middle and high school age children are now more likely to die as the result of a firearm injury than from any other single cause of death.

For Americans between the ages of 1 and 19, a little over half of 2017 firearm-related deaths are homicides.

Another 38% of firearm-related deaths in this age group are suicides, while the rest result from unintentional injuries or undetermined causes.

What's more, the U.S. has had 1,316 school shootings since 1970. The numbers of these tragic events have been increasing, with 18% of the total occurring in the past seven years since the Newtown school shooting at Sandy Hook Elementary School.

School shootings are a focus of media attention and raise awareness about the problem of firearm deaths among children and teens. But they remain the smallest proportion of deaths, accounting for 1.2% of all homicides among 5 to 18-year-olds.

Death Disparities

African American children and teens are over eight times more likely to die from firearm homicide than their white counterparts. Firearms have been the leading cause of death for African American youth for well over a decade.

Firearm suicide rates are highest among American Indian/Alaskan Native and white children and teens, compared to other racial/ethnic groups.

Researchers have limited information on the reasons for these racial disparities. We suspect they are likely a result of a number of factors, including socioeconomic status, firearm availability and accessibility, and lack of access to mental health services.

Although firearm-related rates of death for children and teens living in urban, suburban and rural communities are similar, rural rates of firearm suicide are twice as high and unintentional firearm injuries are four times higher than in urban communities. Meanwhile, firearm homicide rates are twice as high in urban than in rural communities.

A Uniquely American Epidemic

The U.S. stands out among high-income countries: Over 90% of all the firearm deaths among children and adolescents that occur in industrialized nations occur in this country.

Furthermore, the U.S. has more privately owned firearms—not including military firearms—than citizens.

In a Pew Research Center survey of U.S. adults in 2017, about 30% reported owning a firearm and 42% reported living in a household with firearms.

Two-thirds of households have more than one firearm and almost one-third have five or more firearms. Firearms may have different purposes—deer hunting, shooting competition, target practice and so on—which may explain why so many households own more than one gun.

Pew's data indicates that 54% of firearm owners with children under 18 living in the home have their firearms locked away. This suggests to us that young children and teens may have relatively easy access to unsecured firearms.

Digging into the Data

Research on firearms is limited in the U.S.

Government sponsorship of research focused on firearms has been virtually eliminated by an annual appropriations amendment, first added by Arkansas Congressman Jay Dickey in 1996.

Recently, academics, the National Institutes of Health, state governments and private foundations have begun to renew the focus on research to prevent firearm injuries and fatalities. This is due largely to changes in public opinion about firearms as mass shootings keep occurring.

Established in 2017 with NIH funding, the Firearm Safety Among Children and Teens (FACTS) Consortium is one of these efforts, with a focus on conducting critical firearm injury prevention research while respecting legal and safe firearm ownership. We lead FACTS, in which academics from 14 universities from around the country are involved.

Members of this consortium have begun to investigate key research questions, such as the best methods for health care providers to counsel families about safe firearm storage, interventions to decrease firearm suicide risks among rural teen households, and the effect of state firearm laws on school shootings.

Just as other public health problems have turned to scientific evidence to prevent injuries, we feel that the U.S. should use evidence to inform policies that protect children and teens. Much more can be done to address this vital public health problem.

> *"It is technically correct to say that firearms are the leading cause of death for people aged 1 to 19."*

Guns Should Be Controlled for the Sake of Young People

Amy Sherman

In the following viewpoint, Amy Sherman presents statistics that demonstrate the lethal effect of firearms on the population of young people in the U.S. Sherman cites evidence from a variety of sources that support this assertion and concludes that death by firearms has increased and has become the leading cause of death of young people in the U.S., especially among older teens. Amy Sherman is a staff writer for PolitiFact based in south Florida.

As you read, consider the following questions:

1. Before 2017, what was the leading cause of death among young people, according to this viewpoint?
2. What are the top two causes of death for young people as reported in this viewpoint?
3. Which age group has the highest firearm death rates, according to the author?

"Gun violence has surpassed car accidents as the leading cause of death for people ages 1 to 19," by Amy Sherman, The Poynter Insitute, March 30, 2023. Reprinted by permission.

Should Guns Be Controlled?

A woman who survived a mass shooting in Highland Park, Illinois, in 2022 made a passionate plea for gun safety legislation in front of TV cameras after a mass school shooting in Nashville, Tennessee.

After a police official finished a briefing on the deadly school shooting that left three 9 year olds and three adults dead, Ashbey Beasley stepped in front of the microphones.

"How is this still happening? How are our children still dying and why are we failing them? Gun violence is the number one killer of children and teens—it has overtaken cars," Beasley said March 27.

Beasley told PolitiFact that she was in Washington, D.C., on March 24 to attend the Generation Lockdown rally, where activists and lawmakers gathered to support an assault weapons ban, and then traveled to Nashville to see family and a friend. Beasley became a gun safety activist after she and her son, then 6 years old, survived the Highland Park mass shooting during a July 4 parade.

After previous mass shootings, including at a school in Uvalde, Texas, we fact-checked U.S. Sen. Chuck Schumer, D-N.Y., who said that "the leading cause of death among children is a firearm." We rated his statement Mostly True based on analyses of 2020 federal data. The same finding holds true for 2021 data on children and teenagers ages 1 to 19.

Data Shows Firearm Deaths Surpassed Motor Vehicle Deaths

The U.S. Centers for Disease Control and Prevention publishes data on the leading causes of death among different demographic groups.

CDC data for 2021 shows that 23,198 people ages 1 to 19 died in 2021. Firearm deaths, 4,733, were the No. 1 cause. Motor vehicle traffic deaths ranked second at 4,048.

This data is similar to what researchers at the Johns Hopkins Center for Gun Violence Solutions found when they analyzed

CDC data for 2020 deaths. The lead researcher for that report confirmed that the same point held true for 2021.

Beasley told us she is careful to say "children and teens" because she has heard people dispute the statement when someone refers only to "children." She told us she got the 2021 statistic from Everytown for Gun Safety, a gun control advocacy group.

Generally, researchers say they don't include infants in their analyses because of certain conditions unique to babies.

It is technically correct to say that firearms are the leading cause of death for people aged 1 to 19 when they are combined into a single group, said Veronica Pear, an assistant professor in the Violence Prevention Research Program at University of California, Davis.

"This is an eye-catching and powerful statistic, so I get why people use it," Pear said.

But Pear warned that someone could wrongly interpret the statement to mean that firearms are the leading cause of death for each individual age within the 1 to 19 range.

Firearm-related deaths are exceedingly rare among babies and young children, while teenagers, especially older teenagers, have very high rates of dying from firearm-related injuries, Pear said.

"When all these ages are pooled together, the very high rates among teens are swamping the very low rate among young kids, such that firearms are the leading cause of death for the group as a whole," Pear said.

The Nashville shooting occurred at The Covenant School, a small private Christian school serving preschool through sixth grade. If we look at death data for ages 3 to 12, it shows firearms as the sixth leading cause.

However, researchers we interviewed said it is valid to look at firearm deaths for ages 1 to 19. David Hemenway, director of the Harvard Injury Control Research Center, told us there is no official definition of "children."

Hemenway co-wrote a perspective article for *The New England Journal of Medicine* about causes of death for people ages 1 to 24.

"For more than 60 years, motor vehicle crashes were the leading cause of injury-related death among young people. Beginning in 2017, however, firearm-related injuries took their place to become the most common cause of death from injury," the article said. "This change occurred because of both the rising number of firearm-related deaths in this age group and the nearly continuous reduction in deaths from motor vehicle crashes."

The CDC cites the 15 leading causes of death for people ages 1 to 19, but it does not pluck out firearm deaths. This data shows the top causes of death are accidents, homicide and suicide—all categories that include some firearm-related deaths.

The CDC does not classify firearms as a cause of death, but rather as a mechanism by which death occurs. "So, while our data does not allow us to say that firearms are the leading cause of death for this age group, it does show that firearms are the leading mechanism of injury mortality," Brian Tsai, a CDC National Center of Health Statistics spokesperson, told PolitiFact.

Patrick M. Carter, co-director of the Institute for Firearm Injury Prevention at the University of Michigan, and Philip Cook, a professor emeritus at Duke University and gun researcher, both told us they agree it is accurate to say that in the 1 to 19 age category firearms are the leading cause of death.

Our Ruling

Beasley said, "Gun violence is the number one killer of children and teens—it has overtaken cars."

CDC data for 2021 shows that for people ages 1 to 19, firearm-related deaths ranked No. 1, followed by deaths from car accidents.

That's for the age range as a whole; it is not the leading cause of death for each age in that group. Firearm-related deaths are far more common among older teenagers than among young children.

We rate this statement Mostly True.

VIEWPOINT 4

> "Overall, 59 percent of respondents said it was 'very' or 'somewhat' important that elected leaders in the U.S. pass stricter gun control laws."

The Majority of Americans Want Gun Control
Austin Sarat

In the following viewpoint, Austin Sarat analyzes several issues surrounding gun control in the United States. Sarat presents the angle of the political divide, which generally accounts for red states and conservatives being against gun control, whereas blue states or liberals favor it. Interestingly, Sarat describes a statistic which shows that in reality, even conservatives want some better form of gun control, and it is lawmakers and lobbyists who favor unrestricted gun ownership. Austin Sarat is a professor of law and political science at Amherst College in Amherst, Massachusetts. He is the author of Lethal Injection and the False Promise of Humane Execution.

As you read, consider the following questions:

1. As reported in the viewpoint, which U.S. group celebrates gun ownership?
2. How does the rhetoric of gun ownership generally show itself in the U.S., according to Sarat?

"Opinion | No, This Isn't the Moment to Push for Gun Control. But It Can Be Done.," by Austin Sarat, POLITICO LLC, May 26, 2022. Reprinted by permission.

3. According to the statistics presented in this viewpoint, which group does Sarat assert is out of step with the American people?

In the wake of the tragic mass shootings in Buffalo, N.Y., and Uvalde, Texas, America is about to be treated to an unsettling split-screen drama.

On one side, funerals for victims of the Buffalo shooting are being held this week, and families in Uvalde are grieving the horrible loss of lives at Robb Elementary School. On the other, the National Rifle Association is preparing to gather for its annual meeting in Houston, an unapologetic event that the NRA website describes as a "celebration of Second Amendment rights."

It would be hard to find a starker illustration of America's seemingly deep divide over guns, gun ownership, and the role of guns in American culture and society.

President Joe Biden this week delivered a national address calling on Americans to finally do something about the country's epidemic of gun violence and "stand up to the gun lobby." His political counterparts on the right are, as of this writing, still planning to fill out what the NRA labels a "star-studded cast of political heavyweights" at its convention, including former President Donald Trump, Texas Gov. Greg Abbott and Sen. Ted Cruz.

At the political level, the split (and the heated rhetoric) may reflect opportunism as much as core belief. But at the grassroots, it also speaks to a genuine difference in the American experience. While many Americans have had no experience with guns and can't imagine why anyone would own a gun at all, let alone use one, many other people are brought up in families in which guns are woven into the very fabric of their lives.

These different worlds roughly parallel and reflect this country's familiar red state/blue state divide. Montana (66 percent), Wyoming (66 percent), Alaska (64 percent), Idaho (60 percent) and West Virginia (58 percent) have our highest rates of gun ownership; the lowest are Massachusetts (14 percent), New Jersey (14 percent), Rhode Island (14 percent), Hawaii (14 percent) and New York (19 percent).

This divide is crucial to understanding why guns are such a challenge to tackle as a policy issue. It does not, however, mean that change is impossible, or that Americans diverge completely in what they want. In fact polling shows that Americans of all stripes want something to be done about gun violence and mass shootings—and they embrace a range of reforms that would help curb that nationwide problem.

That suggests strongly that there's room for political leaders willing to stop waving their red flags and rousing their bases, and listen. But listen to what? It's a confusing set of voices out there, and in the wake of another tragic shooting, the voices just get louder.

It's easy for liberal advocates of gun regulation to imagine that these moments create opportunities for change. But precisely the opposite is true.

In the immediate term, the coincidence of the NRA's heartless celebration of the Second Amendment and the school shooting will do nothing but further heat up the rhetoric and lead to a hardening of positions.

The all-too-frequent moments when the nation's attention is fixed on a mass shooting are the least likely time for people to be able to think rationally about how to regulate and control guns.

In those moments, gun owners, prodded by the NRA and its media shills, feel threatened and they flock to gun shops to buy still more guns. Research has shown that over the past decade there has been a "statistically significant proportional spike in sales ... in the months immediately following every single deadliest mass shooting event." In pro-gun states, Republican lawmakers have sometimes followed mass shooting events with a loosening of gun laws.

Such a race to the bottom rightly shocks advocates of background checks, limits on assault weapons and other gun control measures. The denialism and defense of gun rights mounted by the NRA and its conservative allies outrages and inflames advocates of gun regulation.

Sen. Chris Murphy (D-Conn.) captured this frustration when he went to the Senate floor Tuesday and asked "What are we doing? ... As the slaughter increases, as our kids run for their lives, we do nothing. It is a choice, our choice."

He was right to call out conservatives who always seem to say that it's not the right time to talk about gun violence or who respond with thoughts and prayers and stoke fear of gun confiscation as the nation mourns more dead children.

But if we look below the surface, we would see that our political leaders and those who celebrate Second Amendment rights no matter what are actually out of step with citizens, both gun owners and those who do not own guns.

Recent national polls show that "Overall, 59 percent of respondents said it was 'very' or 'somewhat' important that elected leaders in the U.S. pass stricter gun control laws."

Another national survey reports that "83 percent of gun owners support expanded background checks on sales of all firearms, including 72 percent of all NRA members."

In February of this year, a survey in Texas showed that even in that gun-loving state, a strong plurality of respondents supported stricter gun control laws.

For leaders who actually want to enable change, rather than just surf a wave of anger and frustration, it's time to cool the rhetoric on both sides and listen to the American people who want solutions to the proliferation of guns and gun violence, solutions that can save lives. It is time to mourn together, and not conduct an obscene celebration of guns.

And when the mourning is done, it is time to honor the wishes of people in red states and blue states and take the action needed to stem the proliferation of guns and curb the kind of gun violence that takes all too many innocent American lives.

VIEWPOINT 5

> "Did the Australian gun ban and buy-back scheme make inroads into the rate of firearm-related deaths? Did it prevent mass shootings?"

Does Australia Have the Answer for Gun Control?

Rick Sarre

In the following viewpoint, Rick Sarre analyzes the actions of government officials in Australia and New Zealand to combat gun violence. Sarre points out that data and research indicate that actions taken by the government in Australia and New Zealand have made an impact and that gun violence has been reduced as a direct result. Rick Sarre is a former professor and dean of the law school at the University of South Australia. He is an active participant in various organizations and activities in law and politics.

As you read, consider the following questions:

1. According to Sarre, when did firearm-related deaths decrease in Australia?
2. What did Australia's then-Prime Minister John Howard do in response to gun violence, as reported in this viewpoint?

"Will the New Zealand gun law changes prevent future mass shootings?," by Rick Sarre, The Conversation, March 21, 2019. https://theconversation.com/will-the-new-zealand-gun-law-changes-prevent-future-mass-shootings-113838. Licensed under CC-BY ND 4.0 International.

3. As argued in the viewpoint, what has implementation of the National Firearms Agreement (NFA) accomplished?

As she foreshadowed in the aftermath of the Christchurch massacre last Friday, New Zealand Prime Minister Jacinda Ardern has just announced a ban in that country on specific military-style firearms. It will soon become an offence to own or possess semi-automatic firearms and shotguns with detachable magazines capable of firing more than five cartridges.

Later this month, the government will consider further changes to the law that will tighten licensing requirements and impose limits on certain types of ammunition. There will be a gun buy-back scheme in place in due course that will provide compensation to those who possess soon-to-be-illegal guns. Preliminary advice suggests that might cost the country between NZ$100 million and NZ$200 million.

Thoughts immediately go to the aftermath of the 1996 Port Arthur tragedy in Australia. Then-Prime Minister John Howard had been elected only six weeks before the Tasmanian horror unfolded. He immediately set in train the gun control measures that no previous government, conservative or progressive, would ever have thought possible.

The government placed a ban on the sale, transfer, possession, manufacture, and importation of all automatic and most semi-automatic rifles and shotguns (and their parts, including magazines). More than 640,000 such weapons were thereupon surrendered and later destroyed at a cost to the taxpayer of around A$250 million.

In Australia today, there continues to be bipartisan political consensus and broad community support for what was titled the National Firearms Agreement (NFA). In 2017, it was reaffirmed by the Council of Australian Governments (COAG).

There has been some criticism that certain aspects of the original agreement have been watered down in some jurisdictions in recent years, but the requirements outlined by the agreement generally remain intact.

Did the Australian gun ban and buy-back scheme make inroads into the rate of firearm-related deaths? Did it prevent mass shootings? Jacinda Ardern appears to be convinced that answers to both questions are in the affirmative. Let's look at the evidence from the past 23 years in this country to test her assumptions.

Gun Violence in Australia Since the Buy-Back

It is unequivocal that gun death rates in Australia have been falling consistently since 1996. Some commentators object to the connection between this trend and the NFA, saying the downturn was simply a continuation of a long-term decline in gun violence generally.

But recent research found that, compared with the trend before 1997, there was a more rapid decline in firearm deaths after the implementation of the NFA.

However, this conclusion was quickly challenged by another researcher, who argued these findings were simply a consequence of the rarity of these events, and that the data were thus skewed.

The researchers on the first paper then set out to test the null hypothesis: that is, that the rate of mass shootings would remain unchanged after the introduction of the NFA. They concluded that while a definitive causal connection between this legislation and the 22-year absence of mass firearm homicides was not possible, there was nevertheless evidence that before 1996, approximately three mass shootings took place every four years. Had they continued at that rate, 16 incidents would have been expected by February 2018, but that pattern did not play out.

The evidence from the National Homicide Monitoring Program, collated by the Australian Institute of Criminology, concurs with the evidence provided by these authors. Its data indicate that the share of murders committed with firearms dropped significantly around the time of the buyback scheme. Indeed, the number of homicide incidents involving a firearm decreased by 57% between 1989-90 and 2013-14.

In 1989-90, firearms were used in 24% of homicides. In 2013-14, the figure was 13%.

Incidentally, in the United States, 60% of homicides are committed by firearms. To the extent that correlations are useful, there should be no surprises here. The U.S. gun ownership rate (guns per 100 people) is more than five times the Australian rate.

Reducing Access to Firearms Lowers the Risk of Gun Deaths

The evidence that countries with higher levels of gun ownership have higher gun homicide, gun suicide, and gun injury rates is convincing. Anyone advocating gun ownership as a means of lowering levels of violence and crime is arguing against the weight of research.

Jacinda Ardern's initiative cannot do her country any harm. Twenty-three years after Port Arthur and the NFA, firearm involvement in homicide incidents in Australia, including the involvement of handguns, remains at an historic low.

While it would draw too long a bow to assert conclusively that the downturn in firearm deaths in Australia can be attributed to the gun law reforms alone, the implementation of the NFA can be closely associated with the reductions in mass shootings and firearm deaths.

The choices made by the Ardern government to eliminate certain firearms from New Zealand to improve community safety are consistent with the long-term evidence from Australia.

Periodical and Internet Sources Bibliography

The following articles have been selected to supplement the diverse views presented in this chapter.

Robert Gebelhoff, "6 Solutions to Gun Violence that Could Work," the *Washington Post*, June 2, 2022. https://www.washingtonpost.com/opinions/2022/06/02/gun-control-solutions-that-work/.

Sean Gregory, "6 Real Ways We Can Reduce Gun Violence in America," *TIME*, March 22, 2018. https://time.com/5209901/gun-violence-america-reduction/.

Ariel Levy-Edwards, "CNN Poll: Most Americans Want Stricter Gun Control, But They're Divided On Whether Guns Make Public Places Safer," CNN, May 26, 2023. https://www.cnn.com/2023/05/26/politics/cnn-poll-gun-laws/index.html.

Jonathan Masters, "U.S. Gun Policy: Global Comparisons," Council on Foreign Relations, June 10, 2022. https://www.cfr.org/backgrounder/us-gun-policy-global-comparisons.

Ronak Mohanty, "Why We Need More Gun Control in the US," the Current Wave, November 19, 2020. https://currentwave.org/why-we-6need-more-gun-control-in-the-us/.

Megan Molteni, "The Looser a State's Gun Laws, the More Mass Shootings it Has," *Wired*, August 6, 2019. https://www.wired.com/story/the-looser-a-states-gun-laws-the-more-mass-shootings-it-has/.

Michael Price, "Three Types of Laws Could Reduce Gun Violence by More Than 10%," *Science*, June 15, 2020. https://www.science.org/content/article/three-types-laws-could-reduce-gun-deaths-more-10.

Laura Santhanam, "Most Americans Support These 4 Types of Gun Legislation, Poll Says," PBS, September 10, 2019. https://www.pbs.org/newshour/politics/most-americans-support-stricter-gun-laws-new-poll-says.

Dakota Santiago, "Gun Control, Explained," the *New York Times*, January 26, 2023. https://www.nytimes.com/explain/2023/gun-control.

Benjy Sarlin, "6 Proposals to Reduce Gun Violence and How They Work," NBC News, February 28, 2018. https://www.nbcnews.com/politics/white-house/6-proposals-reduce-gun-violence-how-they-work-n851736.

Katherine Schaeffer, "Key Facts About Americans and Guns," Pew Research Center, September 13, 2023. https://www.pewresearch.org/short-reads/2023/09/13/key-facts-about-americans-and-guns/.

Anthony Zurcher, "Where Does US Gun Control Go from Here?" BBC, April 13, 2023. https://www.bbc.com/news/world-us-canada-61591236.

CHAPTER 2

How Do Politics Impact Gun Control?

Chapter Preface

Should politicians, governmental agencies, or lobbyists be responsible for shaping gun control? What about law enforcement entities? While gun ownership and gun control are issues that touch many lives, some worry that politicians and lobbyists act against the best interests of citizens out of desire for power or money.

Most informed citizens would probably guess that beliefs and opinions surrounding gun control and the enactment of gun policies follow along party lines, and in most cases, Republicans appear to favor looser gun laws and restrictions, while Democrats favor tougher controls on gun ownership. It is important to note that deep-pocketed organizations and lobbyists have a great impact on politicians tasked with writing and passing gun legislation, along with those voting to keep such politicians in elected positions. This is not to say that there haven't been some bipartisan efforts in the U.S. Congress towards gun control, especially after a mass shooting event occurs.

The viewpoints in this chapter dissect the issue of how politics affect gun control efforts. Readers will consider the effects of arming teachers in schools, along with how the National Rifle Association (NRA) exerts a significant amount of influence on gun control efforts. Readers will also follow various analyses about who is instrumental in passing gun law legislation, what the average American thinks about gun control, and the role of partisanship in this issue.

VIEWPOINT 1

> "Entrenched opposition to gun control laws, even following mass shootings, doesn't come from the power of the NRA."

American Citizens, Not Politicians, Are Responsible for the Current State of Gun Control

Jarrett Stepman

In the following viewpoint, Jarrett Stepman presents an interesting argument that the American people themselves are impacting gun control issues rather than politicians. Stepman argues that Americans have an engrained value of gun rights that evolved from firearm control in the colonial period of America. Stepman also provides an example from historical Japan showing that taking weapons away from the populace leads to authoritarian rule. Jarrett Stepman is a contributing writer at the Daily Signal.

As you read, consider the following questions:

1. As reported in this viewpoint, how many AR-15s were privately owned prior to 1994? How many in 2021?
2. What percentage of privately owned firearms in the world are owned by Americans, according to Stepman?

"Why So Many Americans Oppose 'Gun Control' Laws," by Jarrett Stepman, The National Interest, April 4, 2021. Reprinted by permission.

3. According to the author, what is the real reason Americans generally refuse gun control?

Many liberals are often incredulous that shooting incidents don't provoke larger calls for gun control among Americans.

This was certainly the case after recent mass shootings in Atlanta and Colorado.

President Joe Biden and Democrats in Congress immediately called for more extensive background checks and a revival of the 1994 "assault weapons" ban.

But if the history of the last few decades is any guide, this move is unlikely to dissuade Americans from their attachment to firearms. If anything, then it will likely have the opposite effect.

"Before the 1994 ban, Americans owned approximately 400,000 AR-15s, according to government estimates; today, there are approximately 20 million AR-15 style rifles or similar weapons in private hands," according to *The Wall Street Journal*.

While Americans make up less than 5 percent of the world's population, they own nearly half of the world's privately held firearms, according to a recent Vox article. This is a remarkable statistic.

Longstanding American attachment to firearms is explained away in various ways. The answers usually revolve around blaming the trend on the power of the National Rifle Association, or more commonly these days, "racism."

The second suggestion is particularly ridiculous. More often than not, gun control has historically been used to disarm black Americans in particular and make it less possible for them to defend themselves.

One historian, Michael Bellesiles, even tried to claim that mass American private gun ownership is an entirely modern phenomenon and has little grounding in the founding era. His book, *Arming America: The Origins of a National Gun Culture*, won many awards but was ultimately debunkedand proven to be based on fraudulent statistics.

In general, these theories wildly miss the mark of why Americans have little desire for strict gun control.

Many discussions around gun control in America focus on background checks and the limitation of specific types of guns. However, if one follows the logic that something must be done until almost every single shooting is stopped, then it's hard not to see the end goal as Australian-style gun confiscation, which former President Barack Obama called for in 2015.

Evidence for the "success" of Australia's law is mixed at best and would be an undertaking on a much, much larger scale than what happened in Australia.

In a time of rapidly increasing violence—in part due to the "defund the police" movement—law-abiding Americans are less likely to want to give up their means of self-defense. Politicians, corporate CEOs, and various members of the country's elite will no doubt have little problem employing government resources and private security for their protection under a regime of stringent gun control. But the average citizen will not.

It must be noted that while firearm ownership has gone up, trust in government—and fellow Americans—has been on the decline for decades. And this gets to perhaps the biggest reason Americans are unlikely to accept strict gun control parameters or even more limited gun control any time soon.

Baked into the ethos of the United States is the belief that liberty and the rights of the people can only truly remain secure as long as the right to bear arms remains secure. There is a good reason for Americans to have this outlook.

History is full of examples of governments using weapons confiscation, gun registry, and mass disarmament of the population as a precursor to tyranny. The American Revolution even began with failed British attempts to disarm the American colonies.

Perhaps one of the most illustrative examples is the great "sword hunt" that took place in Japan in the late sixteenth century. Toyotomi Hideyoshi came to power as second of the three great unifiers of Japan during a century of internal conflict and civil war. His story was particularly exceptional since he rose from the peasant rather than the noble samurai class.

Alas, upon achieving victory, it was clear that Hideyoshi would be no George Washington.

Like most great men in history who've achieved absolute power, Hideyoshi became a tyrant who committed a variety of atrocities. He even enacted an edict in 1588 calling for the confiscation of all arms—guns, swords, and pretty much every kind of weapon—from everyone below the ranks of the thin upper crust of Japanese society.

It was justified as a means to control violence and uprisings in the country. The weapons, according to the edict, were to be melted down and used to create a statue of Buddha. A seemingly noble goal with obvious self-interested intent. The truth was the edict was primarily used to suppress any potential opposition to Hideyoshi's rule and to solidify class lines in the country. An ironic move given Hideyoshi's humble origin.

The edict did have the practical effect of reducing a certain amount of violence in the country, but it also ensured that there could be no resistance to tax collectors or the arbitrary whims of the powerful few who ruled. This mass disarmament was the Japanese peasantry's "first step towards enforced serfdom," according to Danny Chaplin, who wrote *Sengoku Jidai. Nobunaga, Hideyoshi, and Ieyasu: Three Unifiers of Japan*.

A Jesuit missionary observer of the event, Luis Frois, described how this once well-armed populace became "disarmed" while Hideyoshi became "more secure in his arbitrary dominion."

The disarmament edict was followed by more repressive laws all meant to control the population and eliminate resistance to the ruling powers. Very soon thereafter, under Hideyoshi's successors in the Tokugawa Shogunate, religious liberty was curtailed as well.

Christianity was eventually outlawed, and missionaries were expelled from the country. The reforms of this era brought a certain amount of peace but also tyranny, religious repression, and social ossification.

The United States, on the other hand, was founded to be a nation of self-rule, on the idea that all men are created equal, and none have the arbitrary right to lord over others. The Second Amendment and the country's gun culture flow from these ideas. Fortunately, under the Constitution, Americans have many checks on government power. Protection of the right to bear arms makes it unlikely the government will ever even attempt to suppress liberty as authoritarian regimes have done throughout history.

This is no "fringe" theory, but a direct result of the founding generation's understanding of human nature, history, and their commitment to creating a free society that could endure for ages to come. Support of the Second Amendment and the right to bear arms is not a call for violence or general resistance to government. In some ways, it's just the opposite. It provides a more secure guarantee that any mass violence between the state and citizens won't happen at all. Americans are unlikely to abandon this commitment any time soon.

Entrenched opposition to gun control laws, even following mass shootings, doesn't come from the power of the NRA. It comes from the foundational worldview of Americans who not only look at gun control measures as unlikely to stop violence, a curtailment of their own means to personal safety, but also fear that they will ultimately be used to undermine liberty.

VIEWPOINT 2

> "In this case, the issue of gun control did not fade from the public agenda after the Buffalo and Uvalde shootings in May. It rose in importance."

Democrats and Republicans Agree on Some Points of Gun Legislation
Monika L. McDermott and David R. Jones

In the following viewpoint, Monika L. McDermott and David R. Jones report on federal gun legislation that was passed in 2022 after mass shootings occurred in Buffalo, New York, and Uvalde, Texas, marking the first major gun reform legislation to be passed in three decades. The authors outline the important points of this legislation and the bipartisan efforts to get it passed through Congress, explaining why this legislation was finally able to get passed after many previous failures. Monika L. McDermott is a professor of political science at Fordham University, and David R. Jones is a professor of political science at Baruch College, CUNY.

As you read, consider the following questions:

1. As stated in this viewpoint, what is one provision of the new gun law?

"Gun reform finally passed Congress after almost three decades of failure – what changed?," by Monika L. McDermott and David R. Jones, The Conversation, July 7, 2022, https://theconversation.com/gun-reform-finally-passed-congress-after-almost-three-decades-of-failure-what-changed-185942. Licensed under CC BY-ND 4.0 International.

2. How does domestic abuse figure into the proposed gun legislation, according to the authors?
3. According to this viewpoint, what political factors helped allow a bipartisan gun control law to be passed at that time?

Gun control legislation almost never passes Congress, even when there is widespread public support for action in the wake of mass shootings such as those in Buffalo and Uvalde.

That's why we did not expect that on June 25, 2022, President Joe Biden would sign into law a bill containing a set of gun reform provisions known as the "Bipartisan Safer Communities Act."

Based on our expertise studying public opinion and the U.S. Congress, here are four reasons we believe some gun control measures got enacted this time around.

Public Attention

Public opinion is fickle. What concerns people on a given day may not concern them soon after, especially if the news cycle loses sight of it.

In this case, the issue of gun control did not fade from the public agenda after the Buffalo and Uvalde shootings in May. It rose in importance. While just after the shootings gun control was not at the top of the public's congressional to-do list, by mid-June it was, rivaling the economy—48% to 51%, respectively—as a top priority. In addition, public support for stricter gun control laws continued to climb in the intervening period.

What happened to increase the public's support and demand for gun control? One of many factors is that Texas Sen. John Cornyn, a Republican and staunch Second Amendment supporter, came out publicly and declared, "I'm interested in what we can do to make the tragic events that occurred less likely in the future." Within a week of the Uvalde shooting, he and Sen. Chris Murphy, a Connecticut Democrat, announced they would start meeting to discuss potential gun legislation. The actual possibility of reform kept the issue on the media's, and thereby the public's, agenda.

Media and public attention were also stoked by an impassioned public plea from Uvalde native and Hollywood star Matthew McConaughey at the White House, which went viral on social media. Additionally, emotional testimonies in a U.S. House committee hearing provided graphic details of the horrific experiences of students, teachers and parents.

Noncontroversial Provisions

The new law enhances background checks for gun buyers between ages 18 and 21, provides money for states that enact "red flag" laws that allow a judge to take away the someone's gun if they're deemed dangerous to themselves or others, provides funding for mental health and school safety, and closes the so-called "boyfriend loophole," which allows abusive boyfriends and even stalkers to have access to guns. How did these provisions get past Republican filibusters, which have stymied other gun reform bills?

One key factor is that provisions like these receive widespread support from both Democrats and Republicans.

Reports indicate that Cornyn, the lead Republican negotiator in the Senate, presented internal poll numbers showing broad support for these specific provisions among gun owners to his fellow Senate Republicans during deliberations. This reassurance of support from their base likely helped sway the 15 Republican senators who ended up voting for the bill. In the end, these 15 Republican votes were crucial to creating a filibuster-proof majority—at least 60 senators—in support of the bill.

While the legislation certainly is an accomplishment, it is a far cry from what large majorities of the public actually want, including most Republican voters. In the most recent Morning Consult/Politico poll, the public expressed strong majority support for aspects of legislation that were rejected in these negotiations. The mid-June poll shows 89% support universal background checks; 81% support a mandatory three-day waiting period; 80% support selling assault weapons only to those age 21 or older and 79% support raising the minimum age for any gun purchase to 21.

So while the law makes some progress, it's not clear whether the public's attention will move on, or whether the public will continue to press for further action.

Who's Got an Election?

Contrary to expectations, the Republican Senate minority leader, Mitch McConnell, gave a green light to the bipartisan efforts for gun control. This was evident when he appointed Cornyn to serve as the GOP's lead negotiator.

McConnell's support for passing a bill favored by Democrats represents an about-face. During Obama's presidency, McConnell discouraged GOP senators from supporting Democratic proposals because it would make the ruling Democrats look reasonable and effective.

Why the flip? This time around McConnell seems to be betting that it is his party that needs to look reasonable heading into the 2022 midterm elections. Republicans only need to gain a total of one more seat to make McConnell the Senate majority leader once again. Close races are taking place in "purple" states such as Georgia, Arizona, Nevada and Pennsylvania. The path to victory in these states goes through moderate suburban voters, who are supporters of gun reform.

A bipartisan gun reform bill may help inoculate the Republican Party and its candidates from Democratic charges of extremism and lack of concern for the safety of American schoolchildren. This thought appeared to be on McConnell's mind when he said shortly before the bill's passage: "I hope it will be viewed favorably by voters in the suburbs we need to regain in order to hopefully be in the majority next year."

Not only does the new law provide cover for prospective Republican candidates in purple states, but it also required few red state Republicans to cast a vote that would put them in electoral danger.

Of the 15 Republican senators who voted for the bill, only two are up for reelection this year: Lisa Murkowski from Alaska, who does not have to run in a closed Republican primary, and Tod Young of Indiana, who had already won his Republican primary by the time of the vote. Another four of the 15 GOP Senate supporters are retiring and won't have to face voters: Roy Blunt, Richard Burr, Rob Portman and Pat Toomey.

Democratic Leaders' Need for a Legislative Win

Democrats, specifically Senate Majority Leader Charles Schumer, appear to have also been rethinking their electoral strategy when it comes to gun control.

In the past, Democrats have often reflexively rejected gun reform proposals put forward by Republicans as insufficient half-measures—even going so far as to vote against them. In turn, Democrats offer up gun control measures they know in advance have no chance of passing, because Republicans staunchly oppose them and will have to go on record as doing so.

Republicans charge that Democrats would prefer to have gun control remain as a political issue to embarrass them rather than to engage in sincere compromise to get something done.

After Buffalo and Uvalde, Schumer faced the familiar pressure from progressives not to settle for what they saw as watered-down solutions to gun violence. Schumer could have once again forced Republicans to vote against universal background checks or an assault weapons ban.

But the context was somewhat different than in 2016.

For over a year, Senate Democrats have been unable to pass any version of President Biden's signature Build Back Better plan, or much of any notable legislation at all. The party's need for some sort of policy win could well have weighed more than taking a principled stance and fighting for a more comprehensive, but legislatively doomed, bill.

Schumer's decision to allow his lead negotiator, Sen. Chris Murphy, to abandon some long-held Democratic priorities in order to compromise with Republicans may have been crucial to the U.S. Congress finally getting a gun reform bill enacted after decades of frustration.

VIEWPOINT 3

> "If Republicans (or moderate Democrats) waver on the gun issue, the NRA will—particularly in the primaries—pour money and resources into the campaigns of opponents who back more lax gun mandates."

The NRA Effectively Prevents Meaningful Gun Control Legislation
Thomas Gift

In the following viewpoint, Thomas Gift analyzes the hold that the NRA has on gun control in the U.S. Gift details how the NRA uses money, politics, and scare tactics to keep Congressional delegates in line with the group's messaging and ideas about gun ownership and gun control. Thomas Gift is a professor of political science at University College London. He is an expert on U.S. politics and his writing and comments appear frequently in academic journals and popular media outlets.

As you read, consider the following questions:

1. According to Gift, which large national lobbying group effectively subverts efforts of gun control legislation?

"Guns in the US: why the NRA is so successful at preventing reform," by Thomas Gift, The Conversation, June 1, 2022, https://theconversation.com/guns-in-the-us-why-the-nra-is-so-successful-at-preventing-reform-184180. Licensed under CC-BY ND 4.0 International.

2. Which group of voters does the NRA target with its lobbying efforts, as reported by Gift?
3. According to this viewpoint, how many deaths had gun-related causes in 2020? What percent were mass shootings?

In the wake of the recent school shooting in Uvalde, Texas that killed 19 children and two teachers, Democrats in the US—led by the president, Joe Biden—have once again called for stricter national gun laws. Yet many experts believe prospects for reform remain bleak, a reality attributed to the overwhelming influence of the gun lobby.

The National Rifle Association promised to "reflect on" the tragedy at its national conference in Houston, Texas, the weekend after the May 24 shooting. Several speeches—including one by Biden's predecessor in the White House, Donald Trump—expressly addressed the incident.

But the NRA has vigorously rejected any charge that its policies contribute to America's gun problem. Unsurprisingly, opponents of gun reform have accused the media and Democrats of "politicising" Uvalde to press an ideological agenda.

The NRA, meanwhile, has continued to advance proposals such as improving mental health responses, "hardening" schools with increased security, and potentially even arming teachers, which leaders claim (without evidence and against educators' wishes) can serve as a deterrent. These recommendations align with the NRA's longstanding message: tightening gun laws would do nothing to prevent mass shootings in schools.

All of this is occurring as the NRA feels more emboldened with the renewed "culture war" focus sweeping America. Although not entirely new, many GOP lawmakers are leveraging gun ownership as part of a "package deal"—along with what they portray as leftist issues such as trans rights and critical race theory—to animate conservative voters. So, instead of the recent spate of shootings causing the NRA to back way from its uncompromising positions, it has instead doubled down.

NRA: An Exercise in Power

The NRA publishes an A-F rating of lawmakers that grades elected officials on their voting records with respect to the Second Amendment, which guarantees the rights of Americans to bear arms. The formula is simple: supporting looser gun regulations earns a higher grade, whereas making it harder to access guns earns a lower grade. For Republicans from conservative districts, where guns are embedded deeply into the culture, any grade below a perfect A+ can hobble a politician's electoral prospects.

Perhaps most importantly, the NRA also flexes its muscles by unseating incumbent politicians directly at the ballot box. If Republicans (or moderate Democrats) waver on the gun issue, the NRA will—particularly in the primaries—pour money and resources into the campaigns of opponents who back more lax gun mandates. Even the threat of that challenge is often enough to intimidate many politicians from defying the NRA's agenda.

Lastly, the NRA also maintains a large, deep-pocketed lobbying arm in Washington that's involved in pressuring members of Congress to resist any legislation that might be construed as even mildly anti-gun. In the first quarter of 2022, for example, the NRA spent well over US$600,000 (nearly £500,000) on lobbying. That number is only expected to increase in the second half of this year amid the 2022 midterm elections as well as renewed demands for gun reform by liberals.

Will of the People?

Data shows that slightly more than 50% of Americans want tighter gun control laws overall. Support is even higher for outlawing assault-style weapons (favoured by 63%), for prohibiting "high capacity" magazines (64%), and for imposing background checks on private gun sales and purchases at gun shows (81%). Although

Gun Safety Bill Signed into Law

President Biden on Saturday signed into law the first major gun safety legislation passed by Congress in nearly 30 years.

The signing comes just over a month after the mass shooting at a Texas elementary school killed 19 children and two adults. That attack came 10 days after a racist mass shooting at a Buffalo, N.Y., supermarket killed 10 Black people.

"While this bill doesn't do everything I want, it does include actions I've long called for that are going to save lives," Biden said just before signing the measure.

"Today, we say more than enough. We say more than enough," he added. "At a time when it seems impossible to get anything done in Washington, we are doing something consequential."

The legislation, which passed the House 234-193 Friday night following Senate approval Thursday, includes incentives for states to pass so-called red flag laws that allow groups to petition courts to remove weapons from people deemed a threat to themselves or others.

In addition, the bill expands an existing law that prevents people convicted of domestic abuse from owning a gun to include dating partners rather than just spouses and former spouses.

It also expands background checks on people between the ages of 18 and 21 seeking to buy a gun.

The National Rifle Association says it opposes the bill.

"This legislation can be abused to restrict lawful gun purchases, infringe upon the rights of law-abiding Americans, and use federal dollars to fund gun control measures being adopted by state and local politicians," the NRA said in a statement Tuesday.

Sen. Chris Murphy, D-Conn., who led the negotiations between 10 Senate Republicans and 10 Democrats, called the bill a compromise right before the Senate vote began Thursday.

"It doesn't do everything I want," Murphy said. "But what we are doing will save thousands of lives without violating anyone's Second Amendment rights."

"Biden signs gun safety bill into law," by Don Clyde and Shauneen Miranda, National Public Radio Inc. (NPR), June 25, 2022.

partisan divides exist, even many rank-and-file NRA members think some gun legislation should be on the table.

Still, these figures can be misleading, for a simple reason: they don't reveal anything about how important Americans feel gun law reform is compared with other pressing issues. When polls ask Americans what the most important problem is that their country faces, virtually no one—often fewer than 1%—ranks guns at the top of that list. So, it's one thing for voters to say that they support stricter gun laws in the abstract, but it's another to actually prioritise the issue at the ballot box.

It's an iron law of governing: politics involves trade-offs. Because other policy areas such as immigration or the economy rank higher in the minds of voters, politicians don't expend scarce political capital on guns. This provides space for a pressure organisation such as the NRA, with its concentrated interests around the gun issue, to have huge sway over how lawmakers set the policy agenda and vote. That's true both at the state and federal levels in America.

Could This Time Be Different?

After a mass school shooting, it's natural to think that "this time is different". We heard that after Columbine in 1999, after Sandy Hook in 2012, after Parkland in 2018. Now we're hearing it again after Uvalde.

The outrage is palpable and it's hard not to think the culmination would move the needle in the direction of reform. The reality? Expect the status quo.

At least 60 votes are still needed to usher any legislation through the Senate and avoid a "filibuster," which allows lawmakers to stall or prevent a vote on bills. Even apart from the NRA's clout, a major challenge is that the gun control movement is subject to what political scientists label an "issue attention cycle." In short, focus on the issue is fleeting. A calamity like the one in Texas gets considerable press for a while but then fades into the backdrop and is replaced by other headlines. The sustained political will needed to pass gun reform simply doesn't persist.

For all the horror mass shootings, most gun violence in America occurs through a "slow drip" of casualties. The Centers for Disease Control and Prevention reports that more than 45,000 Americans died from gun-related causes in 2020, with about 43% being homicides.

But according to the Gun Violence Archive, only about 1% of these victims—just over 500 Americans—died in mass shootings. Most of those deaths never make national news, and regrettably, are too often ignored by the nation's leaders.

VIEWPOINT 4

> "According to a 2021 poll, 43% of Americans supported policies that allow school personnel to carry guns in schools. But if you take a closer look, you see that most of that support comes from Republicans and gun-owners."

Republicans and Gun Owners Favor Armed Teachers in Schools

Aimee Dinnin Huff and Michelle Barnhart

In the following viewpoint, Aimee Dinnin Huff and Michelle Barnhart present arguments used by both opponents and proponents of arming schoolteachers. Both sides vigorously pursue their arguments from the angle of safety. Supporters contend that schools would be safer with armed teachers, while opponents argue that students and staff would face greater danger from having teachers carrying weapons. Aimee Dinnin Huff and Michelle Barnhart are assistant professors at Oregon State University.

As you read, consider the following questions:

1. According to the authors, who favors arming teachers in the classroom?

"Arming teachers – an effective security measure or a false sense of security?," by Aimee Dinnín Huff and Michelle Barnhart, The Conversation, May 27, 2022. https://theconversation.com/arming-teachers-an-effective-security-measure-or-a-false-sense-of-security-183909. Licensed under CC-BY ND 4.0 International.

2. What is one potential drawback of having armed teachers, as stated in this viewpoint?
3. What is one potential positive reason for arming teachers at school, according to Huff and Barnhart?

In the wake of the mass shooting at Robb Elementary School in Uvalde, Texas, some elected officials are making calls anew for teachers to be armed and trained to use firearms to protect the nation's schools. To shine light on the matter, The Conversation reached out to Aimee Huff and Michelle Barnhart, two Oregon State University scholars who have studied the ins and outs of putting guns in the hands of the nation's teachers as a way to protect students.

What Does the Public Think About Arming Teachers?

According to a 2021 poll, 43% of Americans supported policies that allow school personnel to carry guns in schools.

But if you take a closer look, you see that most of that support comes from Republicans and gun-owners. For instance, 66% of Republican respondents expressed support for such policies, versus just 24% of Democratic respondents. And 63% of gun owners supported allowing school personnel to carry guns, versus just 33% of non-gun owners.

The majority of teachers, parents and students oppose allowing teachers to carry guns.

The largest teachers unions, including the National Education Association, also oppose arming teachers, arguing that bringing more guns into schools "makes schools more dangerous and does nothing to shield our students and educators from gun violence."

These teachers unions advocate a preventive approach that includes more gun regulations.

While the public is justifiably concerned with eliminating school shootings, there is disagreement over the policies and actions that would be most effective. A 2021 study found that 70% of Americans supported the idea of armed school resource officers and law enforcement in schools, but only 41% supported the idea of training teachers to carry guns in schools.

In our research on how Americans think about the rights and responsibilities related to armed self-defense, we even find disagreement among conservative gun owners over how to best protect schoolchildren. Some advocate arming teachers, while other gun owners believe guns in schools ultimately make children less safe. These conservative opponents of arming teachers instead support fortifying the building's design and features.

After the massacre in Uvalde, we are seeing renewed calls from politicians to arm teachers and provide them with specialized training.

However, amid conflicting reports about whether police officers engaged the Robb Elementary School shooter, there are renewed questions about whether armed teachers would make a difference. Police have acknowledged they didn't enter the school even as kids frantically dialed 911.

Given that there were also armed officers present at the Columbine and Parkland school massacres in 1999 and 2018, respectively, the public is understandably right to wonder whether armed teachers can effectively neutralize a shooter. Amid reports that trained and experienced police officers may have been unable or unwilling to intervene against the Uvalde shooter, it's not clear whether teachers would be, either.

What Are the Potential Drawbacks of Arming Teachers?

Arming teachers introduces risks to students and staff, as well as school districts themselves. These include the risk of teachers accidentally shooting themselves or students and fellow staff. There are also moral and legal risks associated with improper or inaccurate defensive use of a firearm—even for teachers who have undertaken specialized firearms training.

One study found that highly trained police in gunfights hit their target only 18% of the time. Even if teachers, who would likely have less training, achieve the same accuracy, four or five of every six bullets fired by a teacher would hit something or someone other than the shooter. Further, a teacher responding with force to a shooter may be mistaken for the perpetrator by law enforcement or by armed colleagues.

Introducing guns to the school environment also poses everyday risks. Armed teachers may unintentionally discharge their firearm. For instance, an armed police officer accidentally discharged his weapon in his office at a school in Alexandria, Virginia in 2018. Guns can also fall into the wrong hands. Research on shootings that took place in hospital emergency rooms found that in 23% of the cases, the weapon used was a gun the perpetrator took from a hospital security guard.

Students could also access firearms that are improperly stored or mishandled. Improper storage is a common problem among American gun owners. In a school setting, this has resulted in students finding a teacher's misplaced firearm, sometimes taking it or reporting it to another school official. News reports show that guns carried into schools have fallen out of teachers' clothing, and have been left in bathrooms and locker rooms. There have also been reports of students stealing guns from teachers.

Insurance companies also see concealed guns on school grounds as creating a heightened liability risk.

Other drawbacks to arming teachers involve the learning environment. In particular, owing to structural racism and discriminatory school security policies, Black high school students are less supportive than white students of arming teachers—16% versus 26%—and report feeling less safe if teachers are carrying firearms.

What Are the Arguments for Arming Teachers?

Proponents emphasize that teachers, as Americans, have a right to use firearms to defend themselves against violent crime, including a school shooter. Our research shows that some people interpret their right to armed self-defense as a moral obligation, and argue that teachers have both a right and a responsibility to use firearms to protect themselves and their students.

Parents who regularly carry handguns to protect themselves and their children may take comfort knowing that their child's teacher could perform the role of protector at school.

In a school shooting, where lives can be saved or ended in a matter of seconds, some people may feel more secure believing a shooter would immediately meet armed resistance from a teacher without needing to wait for an armed school officer to respond.

Have Any School Districts Allowed Teachers to Arm Themselves?

Yes. Teachers may carry guns at school in districts in at least 19 states. The idea surfaced as a viable policy after the 1999 Columbine shooting, and gained momentum after the 2018 Parkland shooting.

The number of school districts that permit teachers to be armed is difficult to ascertain. Policies vary across states. New York bars school districts from allowing teachers to carry guns, while Missouri and Montana authorize teachers to carry firearms.

What Were the Results?

There are documented incidents of school staff using their firearm to neutralize a shooter. However, researchers have not found evidence that arming teachers increases school safety. Rather, arming teachers may contribute to a false sense of security for teachers, students and the community.

VIEWPOINT 5

> "Here are some key findings about Americans' attitudes about gun violence, gun policy and other subjects, drawn from recent surveys by Pew Research Center and Gallup."

Facts, Opinions, and Beliefs About Guns in America

Katherine Schaeffer

In the following viewpoint, Katherine Schaeffer details statistics on guns and gun control in the United States collected in a survey by the Pew Research Center. Schaeffer provides facts about gun ownership and gun control beliefs, including who owns guns, why people own guns, whether they believe in stricter gun control laws, whether they think gun violence is a large problem in the U.S., and more. Katherine Schaeffer is a research analyst at Pew Research Center. She previously worked as a reporter covering educational issues.

As you read, consider the following questions:

1. According to Schaeffer, what group of Americans tend to own more guns?
2. What is one gun policy issue that Democrats and Republicans agree on, as stated in this viewpoint?

"Key facts about Americans and guns," by Katherine Schaeffer, Pew Research Center, September 13, 2021.

3. How is the urban-rural divide expressed in gun control opinions, as reported by Schaeffer?

Guns are deeply ingrained in American society and the nation's political debates.

The Second Amendment to the U.S. Constitution gives Americans the right to bear arms, and about a third of U.S. adults say they personally own a gun. At the same time, President Joe Biden and other policymakers earlier this year proposed new restrictions on firearm access in an effort to address gun violence ranging from rising murder rates in some major cities to mass shootings.

Here are some key findings about Americans' attitudes about gun violence, gun policy and other subjects, drawn from recent surveys by Pew Research Center and Gallup.

Four-in-ten U.S. adults say they live in a household with a gun, including 30% who say they personally own one, according to a Pew Research Center survey conducted in June 2021.

There are differences in gun ownership rates by political party affiliation, gender, geography and other factors. For instance, 44% of Republicans and Republican-leaning independents say they personally own a gun, compared with 20% of Democrats and Democratic leaners.

Men are more likely than women to say they own a gun (39% vs. 22%). And 41% of adults living in rural areas report owning a firearm, compared with about 29% of those living in the suburbs and two-in-ten living in cities.

Federal data suggests that gun sales have risen in recent years, particularly during the coronavirus pandemic. In 2020, the number of monthly federal background checks for gun purchases was consistently at least 20% higher than in the same month in 2019, according to the FBI's National Instant Criminal Background Check System. The largest comparative percentage point difference occurred in July 2020—when about 3.6 million background checks were completed, 44% more than were conducted in July 2019.

Personal protection tops the list of reasons why gun owners say they own a firearm. In a Gallup survey conducted in August 2019, gun owners were most likely to cite personal safety or protection as the reason they own a firearm. Roughly six-in-ten (63%) said this in an open-ended question. Considerably smaller shares gave other reasons, including hunting (40%), nonspecific recreation or sport (11%), that their gun was an antique or a family heirloom (6%) or that the gun was related to their line of work (5%).

A Pew Research Center survey conducted in 2017 found similar patterns in firearm owners' stated reasons for owning a gun.

Around half of Americans (48%) see gun violence as a very big problem in the country today, according to a Pew Research Center survey conducted in April 2021. That's comparable to the share who say the same about the federal budget deficit (49%), violent crime (48%), illegal immigration (48%) and the coronavirus outbreak (47%). Only one issue is viewed as a very big problem by a majority of Americans: the affordability of health care (56%).

Another 24% of adults say gun violence is a moderately big problem. About three-in-ten say it is either a small problem (22%) or not a problem at all (6%).

Attitudes about gun violence differ widely by race, ethnicity, party and community type. About eight-in-ten Black adults (82%) say gun violence is a very big problem – by far the largest share of any racial or ethnic group. By comparison, about six-in-ten Hispanic adults (58%) and 39% of White adults view gun violence this way. (Due to sample size limitations, data for Asian Americans is not available.)

Democrats and Democratic-leaning independents are far more likely than Republicans and GOP leaners to see gun violence as a major problem (73% vs. 18%). And nearly two-thirds of Americans who describe their community as urban (65%) say the same, compared with 47% of suburbanites and 35% of those who live in rural areas.

Roughly half of Americans (53%) favor stricter gun laws, a decline since 2019, according to the Center's April 2021 survey.

Smaller shares say these laws are about right (32%) or should be less strict (14%). The share of Americans who say gun laws should be stricter has decreased from 60% in September 2019. Current opinions are in line with what they were in March 2017.

Among Republicans and Republican-leaning independents, views have shifted. Republicans are currently more likely to say gun laws should be less strict (27%) than stricter (20%). In 2019, by comparison, a larger share of Republicans favored stricter gun laws than less strict laws (31% vs. 20%). Both years, roughly half of Republicans said current gun laws were about right.

Today, a large majority of Democrats and Democratic leaners (81%) say gun laws should be stricter, though this share has declined slightly since 2019 (down from 86%).

Americans are divided over whether restricting legal gun ownership would lead to fewer mass shootings. Debates over the nation's gun laws have often followed recent mass shootings. But Americans are split over whether legal changes would lead to fewer mass shootings, according to the same spring 2021 poll. About half of adults (49%) say there would be fewer mass shootings if it was harder for people to obtain guns legally, while about as many either say this would make no difference (42%) or that there would be more mass shootings (9%).

The public is even more divided about the effects of gun ownership on crime overall. Around a third (34%) say that if more people owned guns, there would be more crime. The same percentage (34%) say there would be no difference in crime, while 31% say there would be less crime.

There is broad partisan agreement on some gun policy proposals, but most are politically divisive, the April 2021 survey found. Majorities in both partisan coalitions favor two policies that would restrict gun access: preventing those with mental illnesses from purchasing guns (85% of Republicans and 90% of Democrats support this) and subjecting private gun sales and gun show sales to background checks (70% of Republicans, 92% of Democrats).

Majorities in both parties also *oppose* allowing people to carry concealed firearms without a permit.

Other proposals bring out stark partisan rifts. While 80% or more Democrats favor creating a federal database to track all gun sales and banning both assault-style weapons and high-capacity ammunition magazines that hold more than 10 rounds, majorities of Republicans oppose these proposals.

Most Republicans, on the other hand, support allowing people to carry concealed guns in more places (72%) and allowing teachers and school officials to carry guns in K-12 schools (66%). These proposals are supported by just 20% and 24% of Democrats, respectively.

Gun ownership is closely linked with views on gun policies. This is true even among gun owners and non-owners within the same political party, according to the April 2021 Center survey.

Among Republicans, gun owners are generally less likely than non-owners to favor policies that restrict access to guns. Democratic non-gun owners are generally the most likely to favor restrictions.

For example, a majority of Republicans who *don't* own a gun (57%) say they favor creating a federal government database to track all gun sales, while 30% of Republican gun owners say the same. There are similar-sized gaps among Republicans who own guns and those who do not on banning assault-style weapons and high-capacity magazines.

Among Democrats, there are modest gaps on gun policies by gun ownership. For instance, while majorities of Democratic gun owners and non-owners both favor banning assault-style weapons and banning high-capacity magazines, Democratic gun owners are about 20 percentage points less likely to say this.

Americans in rural areas typically favor more expansive gun access, while Americans in urban places prefer more restrictive policies, according to the April 2021 survey. Even though rural areas tend to be more Republican and urban communities more Democratic, this pattern holds true even within each political party.

For example, 71% of rural Republicans favor allowing teachers and other school officials to carry guns in K-12 schools, compared with 56% of Republicans living in urban places. Conversely, about half of Republicans who live in urban communities (51%) favor bans on assault-style weapons, compared with 31% of those living in rural areas.

Democrats favor more gun restrictions regardless of where they live, but there are still some differences by community type. A third of rural Democrats (33%), for instance, support allowing teachers and other school officials to carry guns in K-12 schools, compared with 21% of those in urban areas.

VIEWPOINT 6

> "*The absence of strict control policies in Republican-controlled states shows that senators crossing party lines to support gun control would be out of step with the views of voters whose support they need to win elections.*"

In Some States, Gun Laws Are Weakened After Mass Shooting Incidents

Christopher Poliquin

In the following viewpoint, Christopher Poliquin suggests that some states in the U.S. actually weaken their gun control laws after mass shooting incidents. While this may seem contrary to common sense, according to Poliquin it is a decision that is largely driven by ideology. On both sides of the aisle, mass shootings have an impact on legislation—they just impact the type of gun legislation that is proposed in different ways. Christopher Poliquin is an assistant professor at the University of California at Los Angeles. He researches and writes about guns and their impact on violence.

"Gun control fails quickly in Congress after each mass shooting, but states often act – including to loosen gun laws," by Christopher Poliquin, The Conversation, March 25, 2021. https://theconversation.com/gun-control-fails-quickly-in-congress-after-each-mass-shooting-but-states-often-act-including-to-loosen-gun-laws-157746. Licensed under CC-BY ND 4.0 International.

Gun Control

As you read, consider the following questions:

1. Which political party favors stricter gun laws, according to the author?
2. What happens to gun sales after a mass shooting incident, as stated in this viewpoint?
3. In gun violence incidents, where do Republicans typically lay blame as reported by Poliquin?

Recent mass shootings at three spas in Atlanta, Georgia and a supermarket in Boulder, Colorado have renewed calls for new gun legislation.

The U.S. has been here before—after shootings in Tucson, Aurora, Newtown, Charleston, Roseburg, San Bernardino, Orlando, Las Vegas, Parkland, El Paso and other communities across the United States.

Congress has declined to pass significant new gun legislation after dozens of shootings, including shootings that occurred during periods like this one, with Democrats controlling the House of Representatives, Senate and presidency.

This response may seem puzzling given that national opinion polls reveal extensive support for several gun control policies, including expanding background checks and banning assault weapons.

But polls do not determine policy. Stricter gun laws are more popular among Democrats than Republicans, and major new legislation would likely need votes from at least 10 Republican senators. Many of these senators represent constituencies opposed to gun control. Despite national polls showing majority support for an assault weapons ban, not one of the 30 states with a Republican-controlled legislature has such a policy. The absence of strict control policies in Republican-controlled states shows that senators crossing party lines to support gun control would be out of step with the views of voters whose support they need to win elections.

But, a lack of action from Congress doesn't mean gun laws are stagnant after mass shootings.

I am a professor of strategy at UCLA and have researched gun policy. With my co-authors at Harvard University, I've studied how gun laws change following mass shootings.

Our research on this topic finds there is legislative activity following these tragedies, but at the state level.

Restrictions Loosened

To examine how policy changes, we assembled data on shootings and gun legislation in the 50 states between 1990 and 2014. Overall, we identified more than 20,000 firearm bills and nearly 3,200 enacted laws. Some of these loosened gun restrictions; others tightened them; and still others did neither or both—that is, tightened in some dimensions but loosened in others.

We then compared gun laws before and after mass shootings in states where mass shootings occurred, relative to all other states.

Contrary to the view that nothing changes, state legislatures consider 15% more firearm bills the year after a mass shooting. Deadlier shootings—which receive more media attention—have larger effects.

In fact, mass shootings have a greater influence on lawmakers than other homicides even though they account for less than 1% of gun deaths in the United States.

As impressive as this 15% increase in gun bills may sound, gun legislation can reduce gun violence only if it becomes law. And when it comes to enacting these bills into law, our research found that mass shootings do not regularly cause lawmakers to tighten gun restrictions.

In fact, we found the opposite; Republican state legislatures pass significantly more gun laws that loosen restrictions on firearms after mass shootings.

That's not to say Democrats never tighten gun laws—there are prominent examples of Democratic-controlled states passing new legislation following mass shootings.

California, for example, enacted several new gun laws following a 2015 mass shooting in San Bernardino. Our research shows, however, that Democrats don't tighten gun laws more than usual following mass shootings.

Ideology Governs Response

The contrasting response from Democrats and Republicans is indicative of different philosophies regarding the causes of gun violence and the best ways to reduce deaths.

While Democrats tend to view environmental factors as contributing to violence, Republicans are more likely to blame the individual shooters. Politicians favoring looser restrictions on guns following mass shootings frequently argue that more people carrying guns would allow law-abiding citizens to stop perpetrators.

In fact, gun sales often surge after mass shootings, in part because people fear being victimized.

Democrats, in contrast, typically focus more on trying to solve policy and societal problems that contribute to gun violence.

For both sides, mass shootings are an opportunity to propose bills consistent with their ideology.

Since we wrote our study of gun legislation following mass shootings, which covered the period through 2014, several additional tragedies have energized the gun control movement that emerged following the December 2012 shooting at Sandy Hook Elementary School in Connecticut. Student activism following the 2018 shooting at Marjory Stoneman Douglas High School in Parkland, Florida, did not result in congressional action but led several states to pass new gun control laws.

With more funding and better organization, this new movement is better positioned than prior gun control movements to advocate for stricter gun policies following mass shootings. But with states historically more active than Congress on the issue of guns, both advocates and opponents of new restrictions should look beyond Washington, D.C., for action on gun policy.

VIEWPOINT 7

> "Despite broad support for the new law, however, most Americans are not optimistic it will do much to reduce gun violence in the country."

Will New Gun Laws Stem Gun Violence?
Pew Research Center

In the following viewpoint, the Pew Research Center investigates several questions and survey results from the public that glimpse into the complex world of opinions on guns and gun control. In particular, it looks at the federal gun control legislation that was passed in 2022 and discussed in previous viewpoints. Despite support for the law, many members of the public question whether it will be effective. The Pew Research Center is a nonpartisan fact tank that works to inform the public about issues shaping the world.

As you read, consider the following questions:

1. Do Republicans think that the new gun law will reduce violence, according to the author?
2. According to Pew Research Center, do Americans think that more guns lead to more violence?
3. As reported in this viewpoint, do opponents and proponents of gun control laws seem to fall along party lines?

"Broad Public Approval of New Gun Law, but Few Say It Will Do a Lot To Stem Gun Violence," Pew Research Center, July 11, 2022.

Gun Control

Americans are largely supportive of the new gun law passed by Congress and signed into law by President Joe Biden on June 25. Nearly two-thirds of U.S. adults (64%) approve of the new gun law, including 32% who *strongly* approve. Just 21% say they disapprove of the law, including 11% who *strongly* disapprove; 15% are not sure.

Despite broad support for the new law, however, most Americans are not optimistic it will do much to reduce gun violence in the country: 78% think the new gun law will do a little (42%) or nothing at all (36%) to reduce gun violence. Only 7% say the bill will do a lot, while 14% say they are not sure.

And roughly six-in-ten adults (63%) say they would like to see Congress pass another round of legislation to address gun violence, compared with 35% who do not.

The new Pew Research Center survey was conducted June 27-July 4, 2022, among 6,174 adults. It was conducted amid a series of mass shootings and rising levels of gun violence in several major U.S. cities; it was nearly completed before the shooting at a July Fourth parade in Highland Park, Illinois, which took seven lives.

Republicans and Democrats differ sharply in views of the new gun law, its effectiveness and whether further gun legislation will be necessary. The gun law, passed with bipartisan support in Congress, draws overwhelming support from Democrats and Democratic-leaning independents; 80% approve of the law, with 51% saying they strongly approve.

Notably, more Republicans and Republican leaners approve (47%) than disapprove (35%) of the new law; 18% say they are not sure. However, Republicans who say they have heard "a lot" about the gun law are less supportive of it than those who have heard little or nothing about the law.

While neither Democrats nor Republicans believe the new gun law will do a lot to reduce gun violence, Democrats are considerably more optimistic about its effect (68% say it will do at least a little to reduce gun violence, compared with 29% of Republicans). Nearly six-in-ten Republicans (59%) say the new law will do nothing at all to reduce gun violence, compared with just 17% of Democrats who say the same.

Democrats overwhelmingly support further legislation to address the issue. Nearly nine-in-ten Democrats (89%) would like to see Congress pass another round of legislation, while 32% of Republicans say the same. About two-thirds of Republicans (66%) say they do not want more legislation.

The survey also finds:

Little Change in Views of Impact of Gun Restrictions on Number of Mass Shootings

About half of Americans (49%) say that if it was harder for people to legally obtain guns, then there would be fewer mass shootings; a nearly identical share (50%) say this would make no difference or would result in *more* mass shootings. This is little changed from the last time the Center asked this question, in April 2021. While about three-quarters of Democrats (76%) say making it harder for people to obtain guns would decrease the number of mass shootings in the country, 80% of Republicans say it would make no difference, or it would lead to more mass shootings.

Declining Share of Americans Say if More People Owned Guns There Would be Less Crime

Overall, the share of U.S. adults who say that there would be less crime if more Americans owned guns decreased from 31% in 2021 to 24% today. In contrast, the share of Americans who say there would be *more* crime increased from 34% to 41%. The share that say there would be no difference remains unchanged at 34%.

Persistent Divide on Priorities for Gun Policy

About half of Americans (52%) say it is more important to control gun ownership than to protect gun rights; nearly as many (47%) say it is more important to protect the right of Americans to own guns. These views have changed little in recent years and remain deeply divided along partisan lines: 81% of Republicans say it is more important to protect gun rights while an identical share of Democrats (81%) say it is more important to control gun ownership.

Widespread Support for New Gun Bill Among Most Demographic Groups

By about three-to-one, more Americans approve than disapprove of the gun bill passed by Congress and signed into law by Biden on June 25. Nearly two-thirds of Americans approve of the bill (64%), with about three-in-ten strongly approving (32%). Just two-in-ten Americans (21%) disapprove of the bill, including 11% who strongly disapprove; 15% of the public is not sure of their view of the law.

About six-in-ten White (64%), Black (63%) and Hispanic (63%) adults approve of the law, as does a larger majority (75%) of Asian Americans.

Majorities of adults across age groups approve of the law, with about two-in-ten disapproving across all age groups. Older Americans (those ages 65 and older) are somewhat more likely to express approval of the law than are younger adults, though this difference is largely attributable to younger adults being less likely to express an opinion (for instance, 22% of adults under 30 say they are not sure, compared with just 8% of adults 65 and older).

Adults with a college degree are more likely to approve of the law than those with less formal education. A slim majority of adults with no college experience (56%) and about six-in-ten of those with some college experience (62%) approve of the law. Larger majorities of those with a bachelor's degree (72%) and with postgraduate degrees (78%) approve. While just 13% of those with postgraduate degrees disapprove, a quarter of adults with no college experience (25%) disapprove of the law.

In both parties, more approve than disapprove of the new legislation, but support is substantially higher among Democrats than Republicans. Eight-in-ten Democrats approve, with just 9% disapproving; by contrast, about half of Republicans (47%) approve while 35% disapprove. Conservative Republicans are split: 43% disapprove of the bill (including 23% who strongly disapprove), and 42% approve (9% strongly). Moderate Republicans approve of the legislation by more than two-to-one: 55% approve, 22% disapprove.

Americans are largely familiar with the new gun legislation: Nearly eight-in-ten say they have heard or read a lot (25%) or a little (54%) about the gun bill signed into law last month; 20% say they have heard nothing at all about the law.

Overall, those who have heard more about the law are more likely to offer an opinion about it, with support substantially outweighing opposition regardless of how much people have heard about the legislation.

Among Republicans, those who have heard or read a lot about the new gun law are more likely to disapprove of it than those who have heard less. About half of Republicans (53%) who say they have heard *a lot* about the law say they disapprove of it, while 44% say they approve. On balance, Republicans who have heard *a little* about the legislation approve of it: 51% say they approve, while 34% say they disapprove; an additional 15% say they are unsure about their opinions of the law.

Democrats are largely supportive of the new gun law, regardless of how much they have heard about it. Still, about a third of Democrats who have heard nothing about the law (32%) say they are unsure of their opinion of it.

Many Supporters of the Gun Law Say It Will Do 'a Little' to Reduce Gun Violence

While most Americans approve of the new gun law, opinions are more divided over how much it will do to reduce gun violence: Just 7% of Americans say it will do a lot, 42% say it will do a little, and 36% say it will do nothing at all; 14% are not sure. A 59% majority of Republicans say the law will do nothing at all to reduce gun violence. By comparison, 57% of Democrats say the law will do a little and an additional 11% say it will do a lot to reduce gun violence.

Among the 32% of the public that expresses strong approval of the bill, about eight-in-ten say it will do a lot (16%) or a little (65%) to reduce gun violence. A narrower majority of those who somewhat approve of the bill (56%) also say it will reduce gun violence at least a little. In contrast, among the 11% of Americans who strongly disapprove of the law, 84% say the law will do nothing at all to reduce gun violence—a view also held by 71% of those who somewhat disapprove of the law.

About six-in-ten Americans (63%) would like to see Congress pass additional legislation to address gun violence, although there are deep partisan divides on this issue. Roughly nine-in-ten Democrats (89%) say they would like to see another round of legislation, while just 32% of Republicans say the same.

Those who strongly approve of the bill overwhelmingly would like to see Congress pass additional legislation: 91% say this. About two-thirds of those who somewhat approve of the law (65%) say Congress should take up another round of legislation on this issue. By contrast, 70% of those who disapprove of the law do not want to see Congress take further action.

Gun Rights, Gun Control, and the Impact of Gun Ownership on Crime

A narrow majority of the public (52%) says that controlling gun ownership is more important than protecting gun rights, while slightly fewer (47%) prioritize protecting Americans' rights to own guns. As in the past, there are deep partisan divides on this question: Roughly eight-in-ten Republicans (81%) say that protecting gun rights is more important, compared with about two-in-ten Democrats (18%). Overall, Americans' attitudes on this question have changed little over the past three years.

Overall, the share of U.S. adults who say that there would be less crime if more Americans owned guns has decreased from 31% last year to 24% today, while the share saying there would be more crime has increased from 34% to 41%. About a third of Americans (34%) continue to say that if more people owned guns there would be no difference in the amount of crime.

Nearly two-thirds of Democrats (65%) now say there would be more crime if more Americans owned guns, up from 55% last year and 51% in 2017.

By contrast, just 14% of Republicans say that there would be more crime if more Americans owned guns, while 45% say there would be less. While the share of Republicans saying more gun ownership would lead to more crime is little changed in recent years, Republicans are now less likely to say that more gun ownership would lead to less crime than in past years (45% say this today, compared with 56% last year).

Gun Control

Periodical and Internet Sources Bibliography

The following articles have been selected to supplement the diverse views presented in this chapter.

Michael Anestis, "How Will Gun Control Policy Affect the Midterm Elections?" Rutgers Today, October 25, 2022. https://www.rutgers.edu/news/how-will-gun-control-policy-affect-midterm-elections.

Ronald Brownstein, "The Real Reason America Doesn't Have Gun Control," the *Atlantic*, May 25, 2022. https://www.theatlantic.com/politics/archive/2022/05/senate-state-bias-filibuster-blocking-gun-control-legislation/638425/.

Stephen Collinson, "Analysis: Three Experts Explain America's Gun Politics," CNN, May 8, 2023. https://www.cnn.com/2023/05/08/americas/guns-politics-allen-meanwhile-in-america-intl/index.html.

Harry Enten, "Why Republicans Feel Little Political Pressure for Stricter Gun Control," CNN, May 26, 2022. https://www.cnn.com/2022/05/25/politics/republicans-gun-control-uvalde/index.html.

Carl Hulse, "Why Republicans Won't Budge on Guns," the *New York Times*, May 27, 2022. https://www.nytimes.com/2022/05/26/us/republicans-gun-control.html.

David A. Lieb, "Mass Shootings Lead to Widening Divide on State Gun Policies," Associated Press, January 28, 2023. https://apnews.com/article/politics-shootings-texas-colorado-045c6a88439907da9895af0ceb0e9404.

Rani Molla, "Polling is Clear: Americans Want Gun Control," Vox, June 1, 2022. https://www.vox.com/policy-and-politics/23141651/gun-control-american-approval-polling.

Laura Santhanam, "Support for Gun Rights Has Eroded After Nearly a Decade of Mass Shootings, Poll Shows," PBS, June 9, 2022. https://www.pbs.org/newshour/politics/support-for-gun-rights-has-eroded-after-nearly-a-decade-of-mass-shootings-poll-shows.

Walter Shapiro, "The Political Perception and Reality of the Gun Rights Issue," the Brennan Center, April 2, 2021. https://www.

brennancenter.org/our-work/analysis-opinion/political-perception-and-reality-gun-rights-issue.

W. Kip Viscusi, "The Ideological Divide on Gun Regulation," Cato Institute, Fall 2022. https://www.cato.org/regulation/fall-2022/ideological-divide-gun-regulation.

Hannah Wiley, "New Poll Shows Californian Voters Fear Gun Violence, But Democrats and Republicans are Divided," the *LA Times*, February 28, 2023. https://www.latimes.com/politics/story/2023-02-28/california-gun-control-laws-poll-voters-republicans-democrats.

CHAPTER 3

Is Gun Control Economically Feasible?

Chapter Preface

Smith & Wesson: $695 million; Daniel Defense: $528 million; Sturm, Ruger & Co: $514 million—these represent reported earnings on the sale of assault style weapons over a decade (2012-2022).[1] Is it any wonder that executives at gun manufacturing companies have every reason to continue supplying gun owners with the firearms they want? Another aspect of this issue is that gun manufacturers provide stable, high paying jobs to their workers and therefore contribute to the U.S. economy.

The other side of the coin involves the gun lobby in the United States and how some individuals in government make large sums of money from this issue. The National Rifle Association (NRA) and other gun companies and lobbies directly and indirectly give money in the form of campaign donations to certain politicians. The lobby keeps track of which elected officials vote and speak favorably for gun ownership and work to undermine organizations and politicians seeking gun control, and in turn helps gun-friendly politicians stay in office with financial or media and advertising backing.

The viewpoints in this chapter shine a spotlight on the economic aspects of gun control. Readers will become informed about the gun lobby and its influence on elected officials, as well as whether gun manufacturers should be held responsible when acts of violence are committed with their products. Readers will also learn if gun buyback programs can reduce violence and the economic effects on communities when mass violence occurs.

Notes

1. Jack Stebbins, "Gun CEOs call shootings 'local problems' and defend 'inanimate' weapons," CNBC, July 27, 2022. https://www.cnbc.com/2022/07/27/gun-companies-made-1-billion-off-assault-weapons-over-10-years-house-panel-says.html.

VIEWPOINT 1

> "From 1998 to 2020, pro-gun groups paid $171.9m in lobbying to directly affect legislation, according to OpenSecrets, a non-profit that tracks spending in US politics. Since 1998, the NRA alone paid $63,857,564 in that category."

Gun Lobby Money Prevents Meaningful Gun Control

Joseph Stepansky

In the following viewpoint, Joseph Stepansky outlines the ways in which the powerful U.S. gun lobby prevents meaningful gun control legislation from passing through Congress. Stepansky demonstrates that the gun lobby provides backing to political candidates that champion the cause of buying, owning, and using guns through direct and indirect monetary contributions. Joseph Stepansky is a reporter and producer for Al Jazeera, writing and producing content on human rights, foreign policy, and conflict.

As you read, consider the following questions:

1. What is the gun lobby, according to the author?

"What is the United States 'gun lobby' and how powerful is it?," by Joseph Stepansky, Al Jazeera Media Network, May 25, 2022. Reprinted by permission.

2. As stated by Stepansky, who are two political figures getting monetary support for their campaigns from the gun lobby?
3. What three groups lobby for gun control, as reported in this viewpoint?

A massacre at a Texas primary school has again drawn attention to the powerful gun lobby in the United States, with Democratic officials blaming Republican legislators for remaining beholden to influential pro-gun interests that advocates say have stalled national gun reforms.

President Joe Biden, speaking hours after an 18-year-old gunman stormed the Robb Elementary School in Uvalde, Texas, fatally shooting 19 children and two teachers on Tuesday, asked: "When, in God's name, are we going to stand up to the gun lobby?".

Former President Barack Obama, who was in office when a gunman killed 20 children and six adults at the Sandy Hook Elementary School in Newtown, Connecticut in 2012, said the US "is paralysed, not by fear, but by a gun lobby and a political party that have shown no willingness to act in any way that might help prevent these tragedies".

Meanwhile, Democratic Chairman of the House Intelligence Committee Adam Schiff tweeted: "Children are dying, and we could do something about it. But the GOP won't stand up to the gun lobby".

What Is the U.S. 'Gun Lobby'?

The so-called gun lobby in the U.S. is a broad term that encompasses efforts to influence both state and federal policy on guns, usually through supporting candidates who have pledged opposition to gun control measures.

It includes direct contributions to legislators, efforts to independently support elected officials, and campaigns to sway public opinion on issues related to firearms. Such lobbying is often carefully calibrated to navigate U.S. election finance laws.

Several investigations have shown that major anti-gun control lobbying groups—notably the most prominent, the National Rifle Association (NRA)—have close ties with the multibillion-dollar firearms industry in the U.S.

The NRA and similar groups often frame themselves as civil rights defenders, pointing to the Second Amendment of the U.S. Constitution that establishes "the right of the people to keep and bear arms."

Meanwhile, gun control groups like the Giffords organisation, founded by former U.S. Congresswoman and gun violence victim Gabby Giffords, accuse NRA lobbyists of solely being motivated by the goal "to sell more guns and pad the bottom line of gun lobby executives."

Gun control advocates have long blamed the lobby's power for the dearth of federal gun control measures passed in the U.S. in recent years, despite a series of prominent mass shootings and a recent spike in active shooter incidents.

Gun control advocates also blame lobbyists for helping to loosen firearms restrictions in Republican-dominated state legislatures across the country.

Texas Governor Greg Abbott and Republican Texas Senator Ted Cruz, as well as former U.S. President Donald Trump, are set to speak later this week at a meeting in Texas hosted by the NRA's Institute for Legislative Action, the organisation's self-described "lobbying" arm.

How Influential Is the 'Gun Lobby'?

It is difficult to quantify the influence of the constellation of groups that make up the gun lobby, which provide both political cache and millions of dollars in direct support to candidates across the country. The NRA, which has run into financial hardship in recent years, has long maintained a grading system for politicians and undertakes advertising campaigns in support of its interests.

From 1998 to 2020, pro-gun groups paid $171.9m in lobbying to directly affect legislation, according to OpenSecrets, a non-profit that tracks spending in U.S. politics. Since 1998, the NRA alone paid $63,857,564 in that category.

Meanwhile, pro-gun groups have paid a whopping $155.1m in a 10-year span from 2010 to 2020 on so-called outside spending, according to OpenSecrets. Since 2000, the NRA has paid more than $140m in such spending, which includes all spending that supports—but is not directly coordinated with—a candidate.

Unlike direct contributions to candidates, there is no cap on outside spending for corporations and non-profits following the 2010 *Citizens United v FEC* Supreme Court ruling.

In 2016, the NRA reportedly spent $50m in outside spending in support of Trump and six Republican candidates for Senate.

The money assured that one in every 20 TV ads that aired in October of 2016 in the influential swing state of Pennsylvania was sponsored by the NRA, according to an analysis by the Center for Public Integrity. In North Carolina, one in every nine ads was sponsored by the NRA that month, while in Ohio, one in every eight ads pushed the group's pro-gun interests.

The NRA's overall spending jumped $100m in 2016 over the previous year with "no politician benefiting more" than Trump, OpenSecrets reported.

Trump repeatedly promised to support gun rights, in 2017 telling the NRA "I will never, ever let you down."

Pro-gun organisations have also paid a total of $54.4m in direct campaign contributions, a category subject to restrictions on donations, from 1990 to 2020, according to OpenSecrets. The contributions in recent years have been almost entirely to Republicans.

The top recipients so far in 2022 in the U.S. Congress were Republican Senators Rand Paul and John Kennedy, who each received over $38,000 from pro-gun groups, according to OpenSecrets. U.S. House of Representatives Minority Whip Steve Scalise received $25,610 from pro-gun groups during that period.

In 2018, during his re-election bid, Texas Senator Cruz received $311,151 in direct contributions from pro-gun groups.

In 2020, vulnerable Republican Senators Martha McSally, David Perdue, and Kelly Loeffler received over $516,000, $307,000, and $298,000 respectively from pro-gun groups, according to OpenSecrets.

How Powerful Is the 'Gun Control Lobby'?

Efforts to legislate gun control on a federal level have made little headway in the wake of the Sandy Hook massacre in 2012, but advocates have pointed to a growing gun control movement that they say could lead to change.

That movement was "essentially nonexistent" in 2013, when efforts to expand federally required background checks for firearms sales failed in the U.S., Senator Chris Murphy, who represents Connecticut, told the *New York Times* in mid-May.

"It's all about political power, and political muscle, and we're in the process of building our own," he told the newspaper.

Meanwhile, lobbying for gun control, while still dwarfed by pro-gun movements, has grown since 2013, led by groups like Giffords, the Mike Bloomberg-backed Everytown for Gun Safety, and the Sandy Hook Promise.

Overall annual spending on lobbying by gun control advocates jumped from $250,000 in 2012 to $2.2m in 2013.

In 2021, gun control groups spent $2.9m on lobbying.

VIEWPOINT

> "The U.S. is saturated with guns—and has become a lot more so over the past decade. In 2016 alone, U.S. gun manufacturers produced 10.6 million firearms for entry into the market, up from 3.6 million in 2006."

More Guns Equals More Money for Gunmakers and More Gun Violence

Michael Siegel

In the following viewpoint, Michael Siegel asserts that the U.S. is overflowing with guns and gun owners. Siegel argues that this trend is growing and will continue to do so because of gun manufacturers and the gun lobby, both of which encourage gun ownership. Siegel contends that this creates a sense that one needs to own a gun to protect oneself, but this proliferation of guns actually causes more gun violence. Michael Siegel is a professor of public health and community medicine at Tufts University. Siegel's work and research focuses on alcohol, tobacco, and firearms and how these impact health and communities.

As you read, consider the following questions:

1. According to Siegel, what contributes to gun violence?

"How the firearms industry influences US gun culture, in 6 charts," by Michael Siegel, The Conversation, February 23, 2018. https://theconversation.com/how-the-firearms-industry-influences-us-gun-culture-in-6-charts-92142. Licensed under CC-BY-ND 4.0 International.

93

2. Do gunmakers in the U.S. have a monopoly on production of weapons, according to this viewpoint?
3. Why do people own guns, as reported in this viewpoint?

Americans have blamed many culprits, from mental illness to inadequate security, for the tragic mass shootings that are occurring with increasing frequency in schools, offices and theaters across the U.S.

Yet in our nation's ongoing conversation about the root causes of gun violence, the makers of guns are hardly ever mentioned. As a public health researcher, I find this odd, because evidence shows that the culture around guns contributes significantly to gun violence. And firearm manufacturers have played a major role influencing American gun culture.

To help spur this much-needed discussion, I'd like to share some critical facts about the firearm industry that I've learned from my recent research on gun violence prevention.

Surging Handgun Sales

The U.S. is saturated with guns—and has become a lot more so over the past decade. In 2016 alone, U.S. gun manufacturers produced 10.6 million firearms for entry into the market, up from 3.6 million in 2006. Pistols and rifles made up about 85 percent of the total.

In addition, only a small number of gunmakers dominate the market. The top five pistol manufacturers alone controlled half of all production in 2016: Sturm, Ruger & Co., Sig Sauer, Glock, Kimber Manufacturing and SCCY Industries. Similarly, the biggest rifle manufacturers—Remington Arms, Sturm, Anderson Manufacturing, Smith & Wesson and Savage Arms—controlled 62.3 percent of that market.

But that only tells part of the story. A look at the caliber of pistols manufactured over the past decade reveals a significant change in demand that has reshaped the industry.

The number of manufactured large-caliber pistols able to fire rounds greater than or equal to 9 mm increased six-fold from 2005 to 2016, rising from just over half a million to more than 3 million. The number of 0.380 caliber pistols—small pistols designed specifically for concealed carry—jumped to over 1.1 million from just over 100,000 during the same period.

This indicates a growing demand for guns with increasing lethality and a design focused specifically on self-defense and concealed carry.

Production of rifles has also increased, rising from 1.4 million in 2005 to 4.2 million in 2016. This is driven primarily by a higher demand for semi-automatic weapons, including assault rifles.

Explaining the Stats

So what can explain the jump in the sale of high-caliber handguns and semi-automatic rifles?

Gunmakers have become very effective at marketing their wares as necessary tools for self-defense—perhaps in large part to offset a decline in demand for recreational use.

For example, in 2005, Smith & Wesson announced a major new marketing campaign focused on "safety, security, protection and sport." The number of guns the company sold soared after the switch, climbing 30 percent in 2005 and 50 percent in 2006, led by strong growth in pistol sales. By comparison, the number of firearms sold in 2004 rose 11 percent over the previous year.

There's strong survey evidence that gun owners have become less likely to cite hunting or sport as a reason for their ownership, instead pointing to personal security. The percentage of gun owners who told Gallup the reason they possessed a firearm was for hunting fell to 36 percent in 2013 from almost 60 percent in 2000. The share that cited "sport" as their reason fell even more.

Meanwhile, 63 percent of gun owners in 2016 reported self-defense as their primary motivator, up from 46 percent in 2004, according to a Harvard School of Public Health survey.

'Stand-Your-Ground' Laws Flourish

Another possible explanation for the uptick in handguns could be the widespread adoption of state "stand-your-ground laws" in recent years. These laws explicitly allow people to use guns as a first resort for self-defense in the face of a threat.

Utah enacted the first stand-your-ground in 1994. The second adoption did not take place until 2005 in Florida. A year later, stand-your-ground laws took off, with 11 states enacting one in 2006 alone. Another dozen passed such laws since then, bringing to the total to half of all states.

These laws were the result of a concerted National Rifle Association lobbying campaign. For example, Florida's law, which George Zimmerman used in 2013 to escape charges for killing Trayvon Martin, was crafted by former NRA President Marion Hammer.

The American Legislative Exchange Council, an association of state legislators dedicated to limited government of which the NRA was a member, has helped push the laws around the country using a model drafted by another NRA official.

It's not clear whether the campaign to promote stand-your-ground laws fueled the surge in handgun production. But it's possible that it's part of a larger effort to normalize firearms for self-defense.

This overall picture suggests that a change in firearm industry marketing fueled an increased demand for more lethal weapons. This, in turn, appears to have fostered a change in gun culture, which has shifted away from an appreciation of the use of guns for hunting, sport and recreation and toward a view that guns are a necessity to protect oneself from criminals.

How and whether this change in gun culture is influencing rates of firearms violence is a question I'm currently researching.

VIEWPOINT 3

> "Overall, it's clear that the gun buybacks in 1996 and 2003 and related firearm restrictions were followed by decreases in overall gun deaths, including firearm related homicides and suicides. What's less clear is the cause of these decreases."

Do Gun Buyback Programs Work to Reduce Gun Deaths?

David Bright

In the following viewpoint, David Bright presents a balanced look at whether gun buyback programs in Australia worked to reduce gun deaths in the country. Using various statistics, Bright contends that indeed there has been a decrease in gun deaths in Australia. Statistics back up Bright's conclusions, but it is hard to determine whether gun buybacks are the direct cause, or whether the combined gun laws have caused the decrease. David Bright is a forensic psychologist and criminologist, and a professor in criminology at Deakin University.

As you read, consider the following questions:

1. When did strict gun laws take effect in Australia, according to Bright?

"FactCheck Q&A: did government gun buybacks reduce the number of gun deaths in Australia?," by David Bright, The Conversation, October 30, 2017. https://theconversation.com/factcheck-qanda-did-government-gun-buybacks-reduce-the-number-of-gun-deaths-in-australia-85836. Licensed under CC-BY-ND 4.0 International.

2. How many mass shootings occurred in Australia before and after the gun laws were passed, according to this viewpoint?
3. According to this viewpoint, have gun buyback programs decreased gun deaths in Australia?

The Conversation fact-checks claims made on Q&A, broadcast Mondays on the ABC at 9:35 p.m.

> Q&A AUDIENCE MEMBER: The government-funded buybacks in 1996 and 2003 cost $700 million. However, research shows these have had no effect in reducing the number of firearm deaths.
>
> TIM FISCHER: Look, the statistics can be looked at as lies, damned lies and statistics, but a fair take on those stats, I think, would lead the average Australian to believe, correctly, there has been a reduction in gun deaths in this country since John Howard spearheaded the firearm agreement between the federal government and the state governments since the legislation passed, since the buyback took place.
>
> —Excerpts from a conversation between Q&A audience member Diana Melham and former deputy prime minister Tim Fischer, on Q&A, October 19, 2017

The mass shooting in Las Vegas earlier this month once again turned international attention to Australia's strict gun laws.

Just days after the shooting, Prime Minister Malcolm Turnbull announced Australians had handed in 51,000 illegal firearms during a three-month national firearms amnesty.

On an episode of Q&A, audience member Diana Melham, who is executive director of the Sporting Shooters Association of Australia NSW branch, challenged former deputy prime minister Tim Fischer on the effectiveness of the gun buybacks he helped usher in as part of the Howard government's sweeping gun reforms following the Port Arthur massacre in 1996.

Melham said "research shows" the government-funded gun buybacks in 1996 and 2003 have had "no effect in reducing the number of firearms deaths". Fischer responded that a "fair take" on the statistics would show there has been a reduction in gun deaths since the reforms were introduced and the buybacks took place.

So, what does the research show?

Checking the Source

When asked for sources to support his response, Tim Fischer referred The Conversation to research published by Christine Neill and Andrew Leigh in 2008 and 2010. Fischer also pointed to an *Atlantic* article, saying it affirmed his claim that "you are 15 times more likely to be shot dead in the USA than Australia on a proven per capita basis."

Diana Melham provided The Conversation with a response on behalf of the Sporting Shooters Association of Australia (NSW), and quoted a study by Wang-Sheng Lee and Sandy Suardi, who concluded the National Firearms Agreement "did not have any large effects on reducing firearm homicide or suicide rates".

Melham also referred to Australian Bureau of Statistics data and an Australian Institute of Health and Welfare report.

Verdict

Tim Fischer was correct when he said there has been "a reduction in gun deaths in this country" since the Howard government introduced stricter gun laws in 1996, and since the 1996 and 2003 gun buybacks took place.

In the two decades following the reforms, the annual rate of gun deaths fell from 2.9 per 100,000 in 1996 to 0.9 per 100,000 in 2016.

Does research show that the 1996 and 2003 gun buybacks had "no effect" on that reduction in firearm deaths, as Diana Melham said? First of all, it's not possible to disentangle any effect of the gun buybacks from the rest of the gun reforms introduced at the same time.

Some researchers have concluded the reforms as a whole had little effect on reducing the number of gun deaths in Australia. But other researchers have concluded the reforms did have an effect.

What we can say with certainty is that in the 15 years prior to the first gun buyback in 1996, there had been 13 mass shootings in Australia. In the 21 years since more restrictive firearm policies came into effect, there has not been a single mass shooting in the country.

What Prompted the 1996 and 2003 Gun Buyback Schemes?

Between 1981 and 1996, there were 13 mass shooting incidents in Australia in which a total of 104 people were killed and 52 injured. This culminated in the 1996 massacre in Port Arthur, Tasmania, where 35 people were killed.

Twelve days after the Port Arthur massacre, then prime minister John Howard enacted sweeping gun control measures.

The 1996 National Firearms Agreement covered a raft of measures, including:

- restrictions on automatic and semi-automatic rifles and pump action rifles and shotguns
- stricter requirements for the registration of all firearms, and stricter requirements for the storage of all firearms.

The agreement also included a national gun buyback scheme, which saw the surrender of more than 640,000 firearms, mainly rifles and shotguns.

In 2002, more national reforms were introduced, this time focused on controlling illegal trade in firearms and restricting the use of handguns. In 2003, another national handgun buyback scheme was instituted.

According to this parliamentary source, the 1996 and 2003 gun buyback schemes cost taxpayers just under $628 million, somewhat less than the $700 million Melham quoted.

So, what does research show about the effectiveness of the reforms?

Has the Number of Gun Deaths Reduced?

First of all, let's look at Australian Bureau of Statistics data on changes in annual firearm death rates, both before and after the 1996 reforms were introduced.

In the two decades following the gun reforms, there was a reduction in the annual rate of gun deaths—from 2.9 per 100,000 in 1996 to 0.9 per 100,000 in 2016.

So it's true that gun deaths reduced following the 1996 and 2003 firearm reforms and gun buybacks, as Fischer said.

But we can also see that firearm death rates began falling before the reforms and buybacks took place, as Melham said. Australian Bureau of Statistics data show that the annual rate of gun deaths fell from 5 per 100,000 in 1980 to 2.7 per 100,000 in 1995.

So it's hard to tell from these data alone what effect the gun buyback schemes and tighter restrictions on firearms had on this decline.

Did the Reduction in Gun Related Deaths Accelerate After 1996?

A number of academic papers have asked whether the rates of firearm related deaths decreased more rapidly after Port Arthur than they were decreasing beforehand.

The authors of this study published in 2010 used "structural break tests" to examine whether there were points in time where the downward trends in firearm related death rates suddenly accelerated. They concluded that there was "little evidence to suggest that [the National Firearms Agreement] had any significant effects on firearm homicides and suicides".

However, other studies using different statistical approaches have reached somewhat different conclusions.

A 2006 paper found that firearm related suicide rates from 1997 to 2004 were lower than predicted by the trends in previous years. This would suggest that the firearm legislation and buybacks *may* have reduced firearm *suicide* rates. Firearm related *homicides* remained in line with the trends from before the 1996 reforms.

A 2016 analysis found that rates of firearm related homicides and suicides "declined more rapidly" between 1997 and 2013 compared with before 1997. But there was also a decline in *nonfirearm* suicide and homicide deaths during that time of a greater magnitude. Because of this, the authors said it wasn't possible to determine whether the change in firearm deaths could be attributed to the gun law reforms.

The Case of Victoria

In Victoria, firearm reforms were introduced in 1988, eight years earlier than the rest of the country, following two mass shootings in the state. The reforms tightened restrictions on semiautomatic longarms, but did not include a gun buyback.

A 2004 study found "a significant downward trend" in firearm related deaths between 1988 and 1995 in Victoria compared with the rest of Australia. Following the National Firearms Agreement in 1996, "similar strong declines occurred in the rest of Australia".

The authors concluded that "dramatic reductions in overall firearm related deaths and particularly suicides by firearms were achieved in the context of the implementation of strong regulatory reform."

Following the 1996 national reforms, the death rate for the rest of Australia dropped to a level comparable to Victoria.

Comparing Reductions in Gun Deaths Across States

There were also differences between states in the number of guns handed in during the 1996 buyback. Tasmanian residents handed back guns at the highest rate.

In his response, Fischer referred to a 2010 study, which compared firearm deaths before (1990-1995) and after (1998-2003) the National Firearms Agreement.

The study found a "statistically significant decline in firearm deaths in states with higher firearm buyback rates." There was a similar effect for firearm homicide rates, though this was less robust due to the small number of firearm homicide deaths to begin with.

The authors said the paper "provides evidence that reduced access to firearms lowers firearm death rates."

However, the authors acknowledged it was hard to work out *which* aspect of the National Firearms Agreement was most effective, and that the results should be interpreted as a reflection of the *combination* of the gun buybacks and stricter regulations, not one or the other.

Conclusions

Overall, it's clear that the gun buybacks in 1996 and 2003 and related firearm restrictions were followed by decreases in overall gun deaths, including firearm related homicides and suicides.

What's less clear is the *cause* of these decreases.

The difficulty is that there's no alternative universe in which the buyback and restrictions *didn't* take place. So it's impossible to rule out the possibility that reductions in gun deaths were caused by factors unrelated to the buyback schemes and more restrictive firearm policies.

Some peer reviewed studies have found that the gun buybacks and stricter regulations led to a decline in the number of gun related deaths—and suicides in particular. Some studies found the National Firearms Agreement overall had modest effects, while other studies were inconclusive.

What is not in dispute is that in the 15 years prior to 1996, there had been 13 mass shootings in Australia, in which a total of 104 people were killed and 52 were injured.

In the 21 years since more restrictive firearm policies came into effect in Australia, there has not been a single mass shooting in the country.

VIEWPOINT 4

> "While Congress has occasionally limited the liability of companies making other products, such as medical devices and small aircraft, the degree of protection given to the gun industry was unusual."

Can Gun Makers Be Held Responsible for Their Products?

Allen Rostron

In this viewpoint, Allen Rostron explains the immunity from liability that the gun industry was granted by Congress. He argues that it is the result of the fact that the gun industry is politically and economically powerful. In the past, a number of U.S. cities filed lawsuits against gun manufacturers in response to urban gun violence. However, Congress decided to limit the liability of gun manufacturers as a result. Until it makes financial sense to support gun regulations, the industry is unlikely to do much to help reduce the risks of gun violence and deaths. Allen Rostron is Associate Dean for Students and a constitutional law scholar and professor of law at University of Missouri, Kansas City.

As you read, consider the following questions:

1. According to this viewpoint, what piece of legislation helps protect gun manufacturers from legal responsibilities?

"Why do gun-makers get special economic protection?," by Allen Rostron, The Conversation, March 13, 2018, https://theconversation.com/why-do-gun-makers-get-special-economic-protection-93241. Licensed under CC BY-ND 4.0 International.

2. Why does Rostren argue that gun sales increase after a mass shooting?
3. How does Rostren think financial pressure can be applied to the issue of gun control?

The gun industry is one of very few industries to have congressionally backed immunity from liability.

As a result, it's been largely shielded from responsibility for the deaths and injuries its products cause, with few exceptions.

How did this happen? And, in the aftermath of another tragic mass shooting, could this protection ever be overturned?

As an expert in constitutional law and product liability, I believe the answer to these questions lies in examining the economic and political clout of the gun industry.

Gun Industry Gets a Protector

The gun industry acquired its protective shield in 2005 after a wave of lawsuits by cities threatened gun companies' survival.

New Orleans became the first government to file a lawsuit against gun manufacturers in 1998. More than 30 other American cities and counties soon followed.

The suits, prompted by the growing epidemic of urban gun violence and patterned after claims brought by states against tobacco companies, initially succeeded by shining a spotlight on the industry. I was one of the lawyers at the Brady Center to Prevent Gun Violence who helped put these cases together. They uncovered evidence about how gun manufacturers could reduce risks by making changes in the way they design and distribute their products.

But then came the Protection of Lawful Commerce in Arms Act, which gave gun-makers a special immunity from legal responsibilities and blocked most of the claims. While Congress has occasionally limited the liability of companies making other products, such as medical devices and small aircraft, the degree of protection given to the gun industry was unusual and didn't create alternative ways to regulate the industry and compensate those injured, as it did with the makers of childhood vaccines.

Good Times for Gun-Makers

Now a string of recent mass shootings, from Orlando to Las Vegas to Parkland, has brought renewed scrutiny to the gun industry's products and practices.

It comes at a time when the firearms industry has enjoyed remarkable growth. In an unintended and sadly ironic way, the mass shootings actually contribute to the industry's financial success.

Gun sales are strongly correlated to prospects for gun control and surge whenever it seems more likely that new legal restrictions on guns may be imposed. And this was the case in 2008, when the election of Barack Obama rejuvenated the then-stagnant industry. Fearful that President Obama would take away their guns, many Americans rushed to stock up on new weaponry. Production of firearms rose steadily throughout Obama's first term, even though he did virtually nothing at that time to advance a gun control agenda.

The massacre at Sandy Hook Elementary School shortly after Obama won re-election in 2012 drove gun sales to unprecedented levels, with production reaching an all-time high of nearly 11 million in 2013—yielding more economic clout than ever before.

The industry's economic impact rose from $19 billion in 2008 to over $51 billion in 2016, according to the National Shooting Sports Foundation, the firearms industry's trade association. And its impact is felt across the country in both red and blue states and politically important ones, from Texas and California to Florida and Ohio. Some of the nation's oldest and largest gun companies are still based in the legendary "Gun Valley" region of New England, but there are other manufacturers scattered around the nation. Wholesale distributors and retail dealers operate virtually everywhere.

The number of jobs supported by the industry nearly doubled to about 301,000 in that period, with the largest totals in Texas and California. The taxes paid by the industry have increased even more dramatically.

The Gun Lobby's Power

Gun companies have made it clear they are willing to relocate their operations if the price is right, and state and local governments have thrown millions of dollars in subsidies and tax breaks at them in recent years. For example, Remington Arms shifted much of its manufacturing from New York to Alabama a few years ago, drawn by $68.9 million in government handouts, as well as displeasure with New York's enactment of tougher gun laws.

And the industry has used this growth in wealth, employment and taxes to exercise its political muscles at the state and national levels. The trade association's annual lobbying expenditures, negligible prior to Obama's election, soared after Sandy Hook to more than $3.3 million in 2017.

Its biggest political influence comes through its customers, who are a uniquely potent force. The National Rifle Association spends over 50 percent more on lobbying than the gun industry and nearly 10 times as much as any gun control group.

And while the industry's interests are usually aligned with those of the NRA, even when a gun-maker wants to take a softer position on gun policy it's extremely risky to do so. A case in point came in 2000, when Smith & Wesson tried to ease the burden of the lawsuits against it by agreeing to be more careful in how it designed and distributed its products as part of a settlement agreement. Its modest steps prompted boycotts by gun owners that nearly destroyed the company in a few short months.

Turning the Tables

The question now is, can the increasing frequency of tragedies like Parkland and the resulting raw youth outrage turn the tables on the gun industry?

Applying financial pressure is one way to get the industry's attention. Several years ago, a coalition of organizations began a divestment campaign, encouraging people to move their savings out of mutual funds that invest in gun companies. Fund managers say the campaign is having its intended effect, with more investors demanding that funds dump gun stocks. According to one study, the amount of assets precluded from being invested in companies that make weaponry for military or civilian use has increased [1,042 percent] since Sandy Hook. This campaign is cited as a factor that led to the bankruptcy of Remington, the maker of the AR-15 rifle used in that shooting.

The idea has recently gained new momentum. Legislators in New Jersey and teachers in Florida are now calling for public employee pension funds to sell their shares of firearms companies. Other socially conscious investors are keeping their shares and using them as a channel to express concern. Shareholders of companies that make or sell firearms, like Sturm Ruger & Co. and Dick's Sporting Goods, have called for gun-makers to explain what they are doing to reduce the risks posed by their products.

Americans fed up with the NRA's intransigence have also begun putting pressure on a wide range of businesses to cut ties with the gun rights group.

What the Future Holds

Preventing some NRA members from getting a discount on a car rental or airline flight is obviously not going to bring the gun lobby to its knees or lead to a repeal of the industry's immunity. But every small step brings attention to the issue and builds the pressure that will eventually change the political calculus for legislators.

A large majority of Americans support the enactment of stricter gun laws, but the crucial question will be whether the intensity of their feelings about the issue ever match the passion of those who fiercely favor gun rights.

Change will happen if enough people make it clear that their preference for stronger regulation of firearms is something that affects how they spend their money and how they cast their votes.

VIEWPOINT 5

> *"I know that the effects of such violence are far-reaching. While the immediate survivors are most affected, the rest of society suffers, too."*

The Social Consequences of Mass Gun Violence

Arash Javanbakht

In the following viewpoint, Arash Javanbakht maintains that there are social consequences for mass shootings that extend to those who survive the violent incident and even those who are exposed to it through the news. These social impacts also have economic impacts on the areas where mass shootings occur. Arash Javanbakht is a psychiatrist specializing in PTSD, trauma, and anxiety. Dr. Javanbakht is also a professor of psychiatry at Wayne State University.

As you read, consider the following questions:

1. What may happen to survivors of mass violence, according to the author?
2. As reported in this viewpoint, are first responders susceptible to trauma as a result of mass violence?

"'What mass shootings do to those not shot: Social consequences of mass gun violence," by Arash Javanbakht, The Conversation, May 8, 2019. https://theconversation.com/what-mass-shootings-do-to-those-not-shot-social-consequences-of-mass-gun-violence-106677. Licensed under CC-BY-ND 4.0 International.

3. Does media coverage play a role in social consequences, according to Javanbakht?

Mass shootings are a tragic new normal in American life. They happen too often, as evidenced by the May 7 shooting in Highlands Ranch, Colo. and the April 30 shooting in Charlotte, N.C., the April 27 shooting at a synagogue in San Diego on the last day of Passover. Schools, places of worship, movie theaters, workplaces, schools, bars and restaurants are no longer secure from gun violence. Families lose loved ones, and lives are ripped apart.

Often, and especially when a person who is not a minority or Muslim perpetrates a mass shooting, mental health is raised as a real concern—or, critics say, a diversion from the real issue of easy access to firearms.

Less is discussed, however, about the stress of such events on the rest of society. That includes those who survived the shooting; those who were in the vicinity, including the first responders; those who lost someone in the shooting; and those who hear about it via the media.

I am a trauma and anxiety researcher and clinician psychiatrist, and I know that the effects of such violence are far-reaching. While the immediate survivors are most affected, the rest of society suffers, too.

First, the Immediate Survivors

Like other animals, we humans get stressed or terrified via direct exposure to a dangerous event. The extent of that stress or fear can vary. For example, survivors may want to avoid the neighborhood where a shooting occurred or the context related to shooting, such as outdoor concerts if the shooting happened there. In the worst case, a person may develop post-traumatic stress disorder, or PTSD.

PTSD is a debilitating condition that develops after exposure to serious traumatic experiences such as war, natural disasters, rape, assault, robbery, car accidents and of course gun violence.

Nearly 8 percent of the U.S. population deals with PTSD. Symptoms include high anxiety, avoiding reminders of the trauma, emotional numbness, hyper-vigilance, frequent intrusive memories of trauma, nightmares and flashbacks. The brain switches to fight-or-flight mode, or survival mode, and the person is always waiting for something terrible to happen.

When the trauma is man-made, the impact can be profound: The rate of PTSD in mass shootings may be as high as 36 percent among survivors. Depression, another debilitating psychiatric condition, occurs in as many as 80 percent of people with PTSD.

Survivors of shootings may also experience survivor's guilt, the feeling that they failed others who died, did not do enough to help them survive or just because they survived. PTSD can improve by itself, but many need treatment. We have effective treatments available in the form of psychotherapy and medications. The more chronic it gets, the more negative the impact on the brain, and the harder to treat.

Children and adolescents are in a developmental stage of forming their worldview and how safe it is to live in this society. Exposure to such horrific experiences or related news, can fundamentally affect the way they perceive the world as a safe or unsafe place, and how much they can rely on the adults, and the society to protect them. They can carry such world view for the rest of their lives, and even transfer it to their children."

THE ECONOMICS OF MASS SHOOTINGS

From 2000 to 2015, there have been approximately 175 mass shootings in the U.S. leading to more than 900 fatalities and thousands of injured people. While there is a growing number of mass shootings, the economic causes and consequences of mass shootings remain unclear. A new IZA discussion paper by Abel Brodeur and Hasin Yousaf documents the socioeconomic determinants of shootings and the economic consequences for targeted areas.

The researchers tracked down the socioeconomic backgrounds of individuals involved in mass shootings. They find that the perpetrators are less likely to have graduated high school than American men aged 20-50. Also, approximately 40% of shooters were in financial distress and 45% were unemployed or out of the labor force at the moment of the shooting, suggesting that economic distress may trigger the rise in mass shootings.

These results suggest a possible role for job-market interventions aimed at high-risk individuals. Notably, non-socioeconomic risk factors such as mental illness and social rejection remain key in predicting violent crime.

Economic Consequences

The study finds mass shootings reduce the number of jobs and total earnings in targeted counties by about 2%. Furthermore, housing prices decrease by 2.5% in the years following a mass shooting. The estimated effects persist for several years after the shooting.

The authors explore several mechanisms that may explain the effect of mass shootings on local economies. For instance, they show that mass shootings lead residents of targeted counties to pessimistic views of their own personal financial conditions and local business conditions. Furthermore, they show that residents of targeted areas are more likely to report being unable to do their usual activities such as working because of poor health. These results provide suggestive evidence that mass shootings may impact local businesses and jobs by increasing absenteeism and possibly decreasing productivity through poor mental health.

Moreover, the authors explore the possibility that media coverage of these shootings might exacerbate the economic impacts of mass shootings. They show that additional coverage of mass shootings in the national media (e.g. ABC or NBC) does increase the number of jobs lost following the incident. These findings raise questions on how mass media should cover these kinds of incidents.

Taken as a whole, the results suggest that the economic consequences of mass shootings are quite significant for targeted areas, confirming the need for public policy efforts towards financial support and examining how to best mitigate the associated risk.]

"Economic causes and consequences of mass shootings," IZA Newsroom, November 6, 2019.

The Effect on Those Close By, or Who Arrive Later

PTSD can develop not only through personal exposure to trauma, but also via exposure to others' severe trauma. Humans are evolved to be very sensitive to social cues and have survived as a species particularly because of the ability to fear as a group. We therefore learn fear and experience terror via exposure to trauma and fear of others. Even seeing a black-and-white scared face on a computer will make our amygdala, the fear area of our brain, light up in brain imaging studies.

People in the vicinity of a mass shooting may see exposed, disfigured or burned dead bodies, injured people in agony, terror of others, extremely loud noises, chaos and terror of post-shooting, and the unknown. The unknown—a sense of lack of control over the situation—has a very important role in making people feel insecure, terrified and traumatized.

I, sadly, see this form of trauma often in asylum seekers exposed to torture of their loved ones, refugees exposed to casualties of war, combat veterans who lost their comrades and people who lost a loved one in car accidents, natural disasters or shootings.

Another group whose trauma is usually overlooked is the first responders. When we all run away, the police, the firefighters and the paramedics rush into the danger zone, and frequently face uncertainty, threats to themselves, their colleagues and others, as well as terrible bloody scenes of post-shooting. This exposure happens to them too frequently. PTSD has been reported in up to 20 percent of first responders to man-made mass violence.

How Does It Affect Those Who Were Not Even Near the Shooting?

There is evidence of distress, anxiety or even PTSD symptoms among people who were not directly exposed to a disaster, but were exposed to the news, including post-9/11. Fear, the coming unknown (is there another shooting, are other co-conspirators involved?) and reduced faith in our perceived safety may all play a role in this.

Every time there is a mass shooting in a new place, we learn that kind of place is now on the not-very-safe list. When at the temple or church, the club or in the class, someone may walk in and open fire. People worry not only about themselves but also about the safety of their children and other loved ones.

Media: The Good, the Bad, and the Sometimes Ugly

I always say American cable news are "disaster pornographers." When there is a mass shooting or a terrorist attack, they make sure to add enough dramatic tone to it to get all the attention for the duration of the time they desire. If there is one shooting in a corner of a city of millions, the cable news will make sure that you feel like the whole city is under siege.

Besides informing the public and logically analyzing the events, one job of the media is to attract viewers and readers, and viewers are better glued to the TV when their positive or negative emotions are stirred, with fear being one. Thus, the media, along with the politicians, can also play a role in stirring fear, anger or paranoia about one or another group of people.

When we are scared, we are vulnerable to regress to more tribal and stereotyping attitudes. We can get trapped in fear of perceiving all members of another tribe a threat, if a member of that group acted violently. In general, people may become less open and more cautious around others when they perceive a high risk of exposure to danger.

Is There a Good Side to It?

As we are used to happy endings, I will try to also address potentially positive outcomes: We may consider making our gun laws safer and open constructive discussions, including informing the public about the risks. As a group species, we are able to consolidate group dynamics and integrity when pressured and stressed, so we may raise a more positive sense of community. One beautiful outcome of the tragic shooting at the Tree of Life synagogue was the solidarity of the Muslim community with the Jewish. This is especially productive in the current political environment, where fear and division are common.

The bottom line is that we get angry, we get scared and we get confused. When united, we can do much better. And, do not spend too much time watching cable TV; turn it off when it stresses you too much.

Periodical and Internet Sources Bibliography

The following articles have been selected to supplement the diverse views presented in this chapter.

Ryan Chatelain, "Studies Reveal Economic Toll Gun Violence Takes on U.S.," NY1, July 21, 2022. https://ny1.com/nyc/all-boroughs/news/2022/07/21/studies-show-economic-impact-of-gun-violence-in-u-s-.

Chelsey Cox, "Everyone Knows the NRA. Who's On the Other Side? These Groups Lobby for Curbs on Firearms," *USA Today*, June 2, 2022. https://www.usatoday.com/story/news/politics/2022/06/02/gun-control-advocacy-groups/7453437001/?gnt-cfr=1.

Tyler Fisher, "The Gun Lobby: See How Much Your Representative Gets," *Politico*, February 21, 2018. https://www.politico.com/interactives/2017/gun-lobbying-spending-in-america-congress/.

Oriana Gonzalez, "The GOP Lawmakers Who Get the Most Cash from Gun Rights Groups," Axios, May 25, 2022. https://www.axios.com/2022/05/25/ted-cruz-lawmakers-money-gun-rights-groups.

Emma Hurt, "Gun Control Advocates Say Culture, Not Just Laws, Must Change," Axios, June 28, 2023. https://www.axios.com/2023/06/28/gun-violence-solution-laws-aspen.

Lauren Lee, "Clarified: Which Lawmakers Benefit the Most from NRA Funding?" KCRA, May 16, 2023. https://www.kcra.com/article/nra-money-funding-politicians/43893650#.

Ivan Pereira, "We All Bear a Burden: How Gun Violence Costs America $280 Billion a Year," ABC, November 2, 2021. https://abcnews.go.com/US/bear-burden-gun-violence-costs-america-280-billion/story?id=80245349.

Dominic Rushe, "Why Is the National Rifle Association So Powerful?" the *Guardian*, May 4, 2018. https://www.theguardian.com/us-news/2017/nov/17/nra-gun-lobby-gun-control-congress.

Priya Satia, "The Hidden Link Between Mass Shootings in the U.S. and the Global Economic History of the Firearms Industry," *TIME*, April 10, 2018. https://time.com/5231027/economic-history-gun-control/.

Amy Swearer, "What Economists Can't Tell You About the Costs of Gun Violence," the Heritage Foundation, August 8, 2022. https://www.heritage.org/firearms/report/what-economists-cant-tell-you-about-the-costs-gun-violence.

CHAPTER 4

Will Gun Control Be Possible in the Future?

Chapter Preface

One could argue that the issue of gun control has meant very different things in various time periods, and this is likely to continue to be the case in both the immediate and distant future. Will attitudes shift to support increased regulation of guns, or will gun rights activists and lobbyists for the gun industry continue to prevent this sort of action?

As demonstrated throughout this book, individuals, organizations, groups, governments, and more have various ideas and opinions about the issue of gun control and gun violence. How can gun violence be stopped? What rights are and are not protected by the Second Amendment? Will we be able to effectively defend ourselves if guns are not readily available? Many times, people appear to follow their political group when it comes to expressing their wishes. But it's fairly safe to say that most people would agree that it's imperative to stop and prevent firearm violence.

The viewpoints in this chapter highlight what can be done for the future. The authors search for clarity and solutions among ideas from various individuals and organizations attempting to help solve this very complex issue and stem the tide of violence. Several viewpoints highlight what other countries around the world are doing in this regard. Others show how many people support taking action against gun violence. Readers will develop a stronger understanding of the strengths and weaknesses of various proposed solutions.

VIEWPOINT 1

> "Twenty-one percent of Americans say either themselves, a family member, or a close friend has had an experience with gun violence in the past five years, and twice as many believe it is likely they will be a victim of gun violence in the next five years."

Americans Are Worried About Potential Gun Violence

The University of Chicago

In the following viewpoint, the results of a poll by the University of Chicago Harris School of Public Policy and the Associated Press-NORC Center for Public Affairs Research suggests a variety of concerns shared by Americans answering their polling questions. The poll demonstrates that Americans are worried about potential gun violence, and some segments of the population are particularly concerned. Various statistics are reported to outline current attitudes of Americans about guns and gun ownership. The Harris School of Public Policy is a part of the University of Chicago.

As you read, consider the following questions:

1. Which groups of Americans say they have had experiences with gun violence, according to this poll?

"UChicago Harris/AP-NORC Poll: About 1 in 5 Americans Say Gun Violence Has Touched Their Lives and Even More Fear Being a Victim," The University of Chicago Harris School of Public Policy, August 22, 2022. Reprinted by permission.

2. What percentage of Americans say that gun violence is a problem, as reported in this viewpoint?
3. Who do the majority of Americans believe should not be able to own guns, as reported in this viewpoint?

Twenty-one percent of Americans say either themselves, a family member, or a close friend has had an experience with gun violence in the past five years, and twice as many believe it is likely they will be a victim of gun violence in the next five years, according to a new study from the University of Chicago Harris School of Public Policy and The Associated Press-NORC Center for Public Affairs Research.

There are significant racial and ethnic disparities in experiences with gun violence. Black Americans and Hispanic Americans are more than twice as likely as white Americans to say either themselves or someone they know has experienced gun violence (54% and 27% vs. 13%).

Looking ahead to the next five years, about 4 in 10 Americans think it is at least somewhat likely that they will personally be a victim of gun violence, including nearly 1 in 10 who believe it is extremely or very likely.

"The poll highlights that gun violence has touched the lives of many Americans, especially Black and Hispanic Americans, and there is significant public concern about this," said Jens Ludwig, a professor at the University of Chicago Harris School of Public Policy. "Despite the polarizing climate surrounding these issues, the poll also reveals strong public support for policies to prevent gun violence, which may help to foster increased consensus among policymakers to further act."

Three-fourths of Americans view gun violence as a major problem, and 8 in 10 say gun violence is on the rise in the United States. Fewer believe it is increasing in their state (66%) or local community (39%). Those living in urban areas (51%) are more likely to believe that gun violence is on the rise in their communities than those living in suburbs (39%) and rural communities (27%).

Many Americans want to both prevent gun violence and protect gun rights. Fifty-two percent say it is both very important to prevent mass shootings and very important to ensure people are able to own guns for personal protection. There is broad public support for a variety of gun control policies, and 71% of Americans say gun laws should be stricter. Majorities favor both policies to restrict who can buy guns and policies banning certain guns, but the most popular regulations are those that limit who can purchase guns. For example, 85% support a federal law preventing mentally ill people from purchasing guns, compared to 59% who support a nationwide ban on semi-automatic weapons.

"The American public is more supportive of policies limiting who can purchase guns than policies banning the sale of certain types of guns," said David Sterrett, senior research scientist with The AP-NORC Center. "The findings also highlight that about half of Americans have intersecting priorities with gun policies, and they don't see a direct conflict between protecting gun ownership and implementing policies to prevent gun violence."

About the Study

This study was conducted by the University of Chicago Harris School of Public Policy and The Associated Press-NORC Center for Public Affairs Research with funding from NORC at the University of Chicago. Staff from Harris Public Policy and The AP-NORC Center collaborated on all aspects of the study. Interviews for this survey were conducted between July 28 and August 1, 2022, with adults age 18 and over representing the 50 states and the District of Columbia. Panel members were randomly drawn from AmeriSpeak, and 1,373 completed the survey. Interviews were conducted in English. The overall margin of sampling error is +/- 3.8 percentage points at the 95 percent confidence level, including the design effect.

A full description of the study methodology for the survey can be found at the end of the report on www.apnorc.org. The proper description of the survey's authorship is as follows: This study was conducted jointly by the University of Chicago Harris School of Public Policy and The Associated Press-NORC Center for Public Affairs Research.

About the University of Chicago Harris School of Public Policy

One of the largest graduate professional schools at the University of Chicago, Harris Public Policy has been driven by the belief that evidence-based research, not ideology or intuition, is the best guide for public policy. For more than three decades, our exceptional community of scholars, students, and alumni have applied this exacting perspective to the world's most pressing problems using the latest tools of social science. Through our undergraduate and graduate programs, we empower a new generation of data-driven leaders to create a positive social impact throughout our global society.

About the Associated Press-NORC Center for Public Affairs Research

Celebrating its 10th anniversary this year, The AP-NORC Center for Public Affairs Research taps into the power of social science research and the highest-quality journalism to bring key information to people across the nation and throughout the world.

The Associated Press (AP) is an independent global news organization dedicated to factual reporting. Founded in 1846, AP today remains the most trusted source of fast, accurate, unbiased news in all formats and the essential provider of the technology and services vital to the news business. More than half the world's population sees AP journalism every day.

NORC at the University of Chicago is an objective and non-partisan research institution that delivers reliable data and rigorous analysis to guide critical programmatic, business, and policy decisions. Since 1941, NORC has conducted groundbreaking studies, created and applied innovative methods and tools, and advanced principles of scientific integrity and collaboration. Today, government, corporate, and nonprofit clients around the world partner with NORC to transform increasingly complex information into useful knowledge.

The two organizations have established The AP-NORC Center for Public Affairs Research to conduct, analyze, and distribute social science research in the public interest on newsworthy topics, and to use the power of journalism to tell the stories that research reveals. In its 10 years, The AP-NORC Center has conducted more than 250 studies exploring the critical issues facing the public, covering topics like health care, the economy, COVID-19, trust in media, and more.

VIEWPOINT

> "The Institute for a Progressive Nevada and the Center for American Progress released a report Wednesday saying the rise of anti-government extremism and white supremacy is being fueled by lax gun restrictions."

Lax Gun Laws are Fueling Gun Violence, and It Must Stop

Michael Lyle

In the following viewpoint Michael Lyle argues that lax gun laws, particularly in Nevada, are fueling gun violence in the state. Lyle maintains that extremist groups in the state are taking advantage of this situation and creating havoc. Lyle reports that gun control groups are active in the state and are attempting to stem the dangerous tide but are having difficulty. Michael Lyle is a journalist based in Las Vegas.

As you read, consider the following questions:

1. Which U.S. state is having problems with extremists threatening gun violence, according to the author?
2. What theory do extremists use as an excuse for violence, as stated in this viewpoint?

"Rise of extremist groups and lax gun restrictions connected, groups argue in new report," by Michael Lyle, Nevada Current, July 25, 2022. https://www.nevadacurrent.com/2022/07/25/rise-of-extremist-groups-and-lax-gun-restrictions-connected-groups-argue-in-new-report/. Licensed under CC-BY-NC-ND 4.0.

3. What does this viewpoint imply must be done to help stem gun violence?

Amid the latest calls by groups wanting more federal and state action on firearm regulations, progressive organizations are laying out their latest appeal for tougher restrictions—make it harder for white supremacists and anti-government extremists to get guns.

The Institute for a Progressive Nevada and the Center for American Progress released a report Wednesday saying the rise of anti-government extremism and white supremacy is being fueled by lax gun restrictions.

The groups called on Nevada lawmakers to ban assault weapons and high-capacity magazines, prohibit guns at polling places, implement waiting periods for gun purchases and ensure people convicted under hate crime laws aren't able to purchase firearms.

Marissa Edmund, CAP senior policy analyst for gun violence prevention and co-author of the report, said Nevada has taken "steps in the right direction by enacting extreme risk protection order laws, trigger activator bans, and child access prevention laws."

"State policymakers must do more to close gaps in state law that allow potentially dangerous individuals to access guns," Edmund said.

President Joe Biden signed gun safety legislation in June in the wake of the mass shooting in Uvalde, Texas where 19 children and two teachers were murdered.

The Bipartisan Safer Communities Act provides funding for states that enact "red flag laws," and closed the "boyfriend loophole" by establishing a five-year waiting period for purchasing a firearm if a person is convicted of assaulting a romantic partner.

While it is the first gun safety measure to pass Congress in years, gun safety advocates as well as Democrats who voted for the legislation acknowledge it's not enough and fails to get to the root of the problem.

Weeks before Uvalde, an 18-year-old white male, who had previously promoted the racist belief known as the great replacement theory—sometimes referred to as "white replacement theory"—killed 10 Black people and injured three others at a supermarket in Buffalo, New York.

"Gun violence prevention advocates had cautioned for months that the dangerous rhetoric could manifest in violent, deadly extremism," wrote Edmund and her co-authors in the report, "however, many did not heed the warning."

The most alarming display of anti-government extremism referenced in the report was the attempted insurrection on Jan. 6.

The U.S. House panel investigating Donald Trump's role in attempting to overturn the 2020 presidential election with the aid of extremist groups such as the Proud Boys and Oath Keepers.

KUNR reported in March that former Nevada Attorney General Adam Laxalt, who is running for U.S. Senate, has embraced support from members of far-right extremist groups, including rural sheriffs clinging to a fringe belief that in their counties they have legal supremacy over state and federal law.

Laxalt has also peddled the "great replacement theory" on the campaign trail.

Nevada, as the authors note, has myriad examples of armed anti-government extremists acting violently.

Cliven Bundy began an armed standoff with the U.S. Bureau of Land Management in 2014. That same year, two police officers were shot and killed by anti-government right-wing extremists who boasted that they had been involved in the confrontation with federal officials.

Annette Magnus, the executive director for Battle Born Progress, and also a co-author of the report, said Nevada is already "seeing how the anti-public lands and anti-government movement has bled into today's violent, white supremacist extremism."

"Combined with how easy it is to access firearms in Nevada, this has already been shown to have devastating impacts in the state, including mass shootings, gun homicides, and violence against police officers," she said.

The report comes at the same time some congressional Democrats are attempting to revive a ban on certain semi-automatic weapons.

The U.S. House Judiciary Committee voted on a recent bill placing a ban on assault weapons, but it remains to be seen if there are enough votes to advance the legislation further.

U.S. Rep. Susie Lee told Nevada Current in May she wasn't sure efforts to ban assault weapons "would get past the House right now, sadly."

Authors of the report are hoping Nevada lawmakers could also put forward more legislation addressing gun violence.

Nevada, they said, has made improvements that include strengthening background checks on gun sales, but the state doesn't "regulate assault weapons or high-capacity magazines, and individuals with misdemeanor hate crimes are still able to purchase a gun."

Giffords Law Center to Prevent Gun Violence gives Nevada a C+ rating when it comes to gun laws.

According to the report, in Nevada "individuals with misdemeanor hate crimes are still able to purchase a gun."

"This is particularly troubling because many anti-government and right-wing extremists have been known to stockpile weapons and ammunition," the authors wrote.

Aside from preventing extremists groups from accessing guns, the report notes Nevada has the 18th highest rate of firearm-related deaths in the country with 17 gun deaths per 100,000.

The Giffords Law Center to Prevent Gun Violence gives Nevada a C+ rating when it comes to gun laws.

The groups argue that implementing longer wait times between when a person purchases a firearm and acquires the gun could prevent "rage-fueled homicides," and banning guns at polling places would protect residents from voter intimidation.

VIEWPOINT 3

> "Studies published in peer-reviewed journals indicate that the introduction of more stringent firearms controls has the potential to bring about a reduction, or an accelerated reduction in firearm homicides."

Gun Laws Must Be Strengthened

Guy Lamb

In the following viewpoint, Guy Lamb analyzes the gun control policies that guide South African legislation. Lamb defines the laws of South Africa and dissects their positive and negative effects on the country and its citizens. The most influential of these acts of legislation is the Firearms Control Act of 2004. The public has debated the extent to which it has helped curb gun violence, but Lamb asserts that data suggests it has had a beneficial impact. Guy Lamb is a criminologist and lecturer in the political science department at the University of Stellenbosch in Cape Town, South Africa.

As you read, consider the following questions:

1. What three things must a person do to get a firearm license in South Africa, according to this viewpoint?

"Gun control in South Africa: tightening the law, and more," by Guy Lamb, The Conversation, August 19, 2021. https://theconversation.com/gun-control-in-south-africa-tightening-the-law-and-more-166194. Licensed under CC-BY-ND 4.0 International.

2. Do strict laws appear to help control violence, according to the author?
3. What types of firearms are used most often in violent acts, according to Lamb?

Statistics produced by the police and mortuary surveillance systems in South Africa have consistently shown that firearms are the most commonly used weapons to commit murder and other violent crimes, such as carjacking and house robberies.

With this in mind, the Civilian Secretariat for Police Services which serves as the technical advisory agency to the Minister of Police, wants to have the Firearms Control Act amended to introduce more stringent firearm licensing measures. The proposed amendments seek to reduce the number of new licensed firearms in circulation. Significantly, if the amendments become law, it will no longer be possible to acquire a firearm licence for self defence purposes.

South Africa already has relatively strict firearms control legislation. The Firearms Control Act, 2004, replaced the 1968 law, which permitted relatively widespread access to legal firearms.

The current Act requires firearm license applicants to undergo detailed background checks and pass a firearm competency test. In addition, only those 21 years or older can apply for a license. And, applications generally have to be accompanied by compelling motivations.

The proposed amendments have once again stirred public debate, particularly about whether tighter laws do actually reduce firearm violence. The Civilian Secretariat for Police Services has invited public comment on the proposed amendments, and has reportedly received more than 100 000 submissions.

Groups lobbying for tighter controls, such as Gun Free South Africa argue that the Firearms Act has been a game-changer for reducing firearm violence in South Africa. They point to the fact that the firearm murder rate declined by 40% between 1998 and 2007. The last amendments were passed midway, in 2004.

For their part, pro-gun groups claim that the firearm law has had a negligible impact on crime in South Africa.

Differing views have also been expressed by researchers. Public health studies have suggested that reductions in murders in urban areas, femicides and gunshot injuries in children can be attributed to the Firearms Control Act.

Conversely, a report by researchers at the Wits University School of Governance "found no evidence for the causal relation between the FCA and reduced crime levels".

I have more than 20 years of arms control research experience, which included consulting to the United Nations, as well as various policing agencies on various occasions. Drawing from this, it is my view that there are two aspects of firearms control in South Africa that have often been neglected in this debate.

These are essential to understanding the relationship between the Firearms Act, and variations in firearm crime. Firstly, that the Act can only have a direct impact on certain types of firearm violence. Secondly, that changes to the law have been one of a number of interconnected measures that the government has pursued to address gun violence since the late 1990s.

What's in Place?

The basic premise underlying most restrictions and controls relating to legal gun ownership is that some individuals are more prone to violence than others. Hence, throughout the world, many governments use legislation to prohibit those with histories of violence, substance abuse as well as criminal records from acquiring firearm licenses.

Studies published in peer-reviewed journals indicate that the introduction of more stringent firearms controls has the potential to bring about a reduction, or an accelerated reduction in firearm homicides. For example, a systematic review of 130 studies from ten countries on the public health impact of firearms control legislation found a significant link between the "simultaneous implementation of laws targeting multiple firearms restrictions", and reductions in firearm deaths.

South Africa, unfortunately, doesn't have data that definitively determine the impact of the Firearms Control Act on levels of violence. But it's highly unlikely that the measures contained in the act would not have resulted in some form of a reduction in gun violence.

These include a requirement that the police perform extensive background checks on firearm licence applicants. This has resulted in thousands of applications being rejected.

The Act also makes provision for the invalidation of firearm licenses in circumstances where owners have been convicted of violent crime. And owners are required to store their firearms in a safe when they are not carrying them.

But there are caveats. One is illegal firearms, an area in which the Firearms Control Act has serious limitations.

Licensed versus Illegal Guns

Illegal guns have been predominantly used in firearm murders and other types of violent crimes in South Africa.

In a paper written three years ago I examined whether there was a relationship between murder and the policing of illegal firearms by the South African Police Service, particularly in high crime areas.

I found that the vast majority of illegal guns in circulation in South Africa were originally licensed to civilians and private security companies. These ended up in the hands of the criminal sector through loss and theft.

Although the ambit of the law can't control these guns once they're no longer in the regulated frame, there is nevertheless evidence that the Act can help reduce the diversion of legal weapons into the hands of criminals. This is because a correspondence has been shown between substantial reductions in the approval of civilian firearm licenses and a significant decline in the loss or theft of licensed civilian firearms.

This came through clearly in a report compiled by the Western Cape provincial government based, on data from the police between 2004/04 and 2008/09.

Beyond Controlling Guns

The Firearms Control Act has been one of many firearm violence reduction measures in South Africa.

One has entailed the police prioritising the seizure and destruction of illegal firearms—both within the country and in neighbouring Mozambique.

The police have reported that they destroyed 1,189,884 firearms between 1998/99 and 2013/14.

There have also been large scale police operations in high crime areas, which have involved the deployment of military personnel with the objective of confiscating as many illegal firearms as possible, and arresting those in possession of such weapons. My own research has shown that these have been particularly effective at reducing levels of firearm violence.

> # WHAT CAN MAKE GUN CONTROL WORK?
>
> ### What Works: Gun Violence Prediction and Prevention at the Individual Level
>
> Although it is important to recognize that most people suffering from a mental illness are not dangerous, for those persons at risk for violence due to mental illness, suicidal thoughts, or feelings of desperation, mental health treatment can often prevent gun violence. Policies and programs that identify and provide treatment for all persons suffering from a mental illness should be a national priority. Urgent attention must be paid to the current level of access to mental health services in the United States; such access is woefully insufficient. Additionally, it should be noted that behavioral threat assessment is becoming a standard of care for preventing violence in schools, colleges, and the workplace and against government and other public officials. Threat assessment teams gather and analyze information

to assess if a person poses a threat of violence or self-harm, and if so, take steps to intervene.

What Works: Gun Violence Prevention at the Community Level

Prevention of violence occurs along a continuum that begins in early childhood with programs to help parents raise emotionally healthy children and ends with efforts to identify and intervene with troubled individuals who are threatening violence. The mental health community must take the lead in advocating for community-based collaborative problem-solving models to address the prevention of gun violence. Such models should blend prevention strategies in an effort to overcome the tendency within many community service systems to operate in silos. There has been some success with community-based programs involving police training in crisis intervention and with community members trained in mental health first aid. These programs need further piloting and study so they can be expanded to additional communities as appropriate. In addition, public health messaging campaigns on safe gun storage are needed. The practice of keeping all firearms appropriately stored and locked must become the only socially acceptable norm.

What Works: Policies to Reduce Gun Violence

The use of a gun greatly increases the odds that violence will lead to a fatality: This problem calls for urgent action. Firearm prohibitions for high-risk groups—domestic violence offenders, persons convicted of violent misdemeanor crimes, and individuals with mental illness who have been adjudicated as being a threat to themselves or to others—have been shown to reduce violence. The licensing of handgun purchasers, background check requirements for all gun sales, and close oversight of retail gun sellers can reduce the diversion of guns to criminals. Reducing the incidence of gun violence will require interventions through multiple systems, including legal, public health, public safety, community, and health. Increasing the availability of data and funding will help inform and evaluate policies designed to reduce gun violence.

"Can gun violence be traced back to socioeconomic root causes?," by Roberto Molar Candanosa, Northeastern University, January 6, 2020.

Firearm Violence Remains a Problem

Despite these police interventions and the introduction of more stringent firearm licensing controls in 2004, South Africa is still affected by high levels of firearm violence.

The annual number of murders in South Africa has increased by 37% since 2011/12, with firearms featuring prominently in the perpetration of these murders.

It is in the best interests of all people who live in South Africa for the government to pursue more effective ways to reduce firearm crimes. More concerted efforts by the police to seize illegal firearms is essential. Improving firearms control legislation is clearly one such needed intervention to prevent the further diversion of legal guns into the hands of criminals.

VIEWPOINT 4

> "Many gun control advocates say the United States should look to the experiences of wealthy democratic peers that have instituted tighter restrictions to curb gun violence."

Following the Examples of Other Nations Can Help Tackle Gun Violence

Jonathan Masters

In the following viewpoint, Jonathan Masters asserts that the United States has the highest gun homicide rate among developed nations. Masters provides statistical evidence to back up his claim and analyzes how other developed nations have been successful in tackling their gun violence issues. Jonathan Masters is a deputy managing editor at the Council on Foreign Relations and leads a team which writes and produces a wide range of content on international relations.

As you read, consider the following questions:

1. According to this viewpoint, what is the leading cause of death for children and young adults in the United States?
2. Which of the world's most developed nations has the highest firearm homicide rate, as reported by Masters?

"How does U.S. gun policy compare with the rest of the world?," by Jonathan Masters, PBS NewsHour Productions, June 13, 2022. Reprinted by permission.

3. What is one way that Canada, Australia, Israel, the United Kingdom, Norway, and Japan prevent a high firearm homicide rate, as stated by the author?

The debate over gun control in the United States has waxed and waned over the years, stirred by frequent mass shootings in civilian settings. Gun violence is the leading cause of death for children and young adults in the United States. In particular, the ready availability of assault weapons and ammunition has provoked national discussion after multiple mass shootings of school children, most recently in Uvalde, Texas. However, Congress has repeatedly been unable to pass meaningful gun legislation in the wake of these tragedies despite broad public support for new restrictions.

Recent years have seen some of the worst gun violence in U.S. history. In 2021, guns killed more than forty-five thousand Americans, the highest toll in decades; and the upward trend is on track to continue.

Many gun control advocates say the United States should look to the experiences of wealthy democratic peers that have instituted tighter restrictions to curb gun violence.

United States

Gun ownership in the United States is rooted in the Second Amendment of the Constitution: "A well-regulated Militia, being necessary to the security of a free State, the right of the people to keep and bear Arms, shall not be infringed."

The United States, with less than 5 percent of the world's population, has 46 percent of the world's civilian-owned guns, according to the most recent report by the Switzerland-based Small Arms Survey (2018). It ranks number one in firearms per capita. The United States also has the highest homicide-by-firearm rate of the world's most-developed nations. Many gun rights proponents say these statistics do not indicate a causal relationship.

However, the right to bear arms is not unlimited. The U.S. Congress and state legislatures have authority to enact controlling legislation, and the U.S. Supreme Court has upheld some firearms restrictions, such as bans on concealed weapons and on the possession of certain types of weapons, as well as prohibitions on the sale of guns to certain categories of people. The Gun Control Act of 1968 prohibits individuals under eighteen years of age, convicted criminals, the mentally disabled, dishonorably discharged military personnel, and others from purchasing firearms. In 1993, the Brady Handgun Violence Prevention Act mandated background checks for all unlicensed individuals purchasing a firearm from a federally authorized dealer.

But some gun laws have not survived judicial review. For instance, in 2008, the Supreme Court struck down a Washington, DC, law that banned handguns, the court's first ruling on the Second Amendment in nearly seventy years.

Federal law provides the basis for firearms regulation in the United States, but states and cities can impose further restrictions. Some studies have indicated that states with more restrictive gun laws, such as California or Hawaii, have lower incidences of gun deaths, although researchers say more analysis is needed.

In recent years, Congress has debated changes to existing gun laws, typically in the immediate aftermath of a high-profile mass shooting, such as that in Las Vegas in 2017 (sixty people killed), or in Parkland, Florida, in 2018 (seventeen killed). But in almost every instance, legislation has failed to garner enough support. Ill-fated bills have proposed measures including an assault weapons ban, expanded background checks, and a prohibition on firearm sales to people on federal terrorism watch lists.

As of mid-2022, there were no federal laws banning semiautomatic assault weapons, military-style .50 caliber rifles, handguns, or large-capacity magazines. There was also no federal requirement for those purchasing a gun to have any firearm safety training. There was a federal prohibition on assault weapons and

Gun Control

on large-capacity magazines between 1994 and 2004, but Congress allowed these restrictions to expire.

Meanwhile, gun violence has surged amid the COVID-19 pandemic. As of June 2022, guns have killed some nineteen thousand people in the United States this year. The majority of those were in acts of suicide. Mass shootings—those with at least four victims—were occurring at a rate of at least one per day.

Canada

Gun ownership is also relatively high in Canada, at about thirty-five firearms per hundred residents (ranking fifth globally), but the country does not struggle with a similar level of gun violence. As in the United States, Canada's national government sets gun restrictions that the provinces, territories, and municipalities can supplement. And like its southern neighbor, Canada's gun laws have often been prompted by gun violence. In 1989, a student armed with a semiautomatic rifle killed fourteen students and injured more than a dozen others at a Montreal engineering school. The incident is widely credited with driving major gun reforms that imposed a twenty-eight-day waiting period for purchases; mandatory safety training courses; more detailed background checks; bans on large-capacity magazines; and bans or greater restrictions on military-style firearms and ammunition.

Firearms in Canada are divided into three classes: nonrestricted weapons, such as ordinary rifles and shotguns; restricted, such as handguns and semiautomatic rifles or shotguns; and prohibited, such as automatic weapons. It is illegal to own a fully automatic weapon unless it was registered before 1978.

Changes to the law in 1995 required individuals to obtain a license to buy guns and ammunition, as well as register all firearms. However, in 2012, the requirement to register nonrestricted guns was dropped, and related public records were expunged. Following another mass shooting, at a Quebec City mosque in 2017, the government passed a bill to again require nonrestricted firearms to be registered and allow background checks to consider events from more than five years in the past. In 2020, after a gunman killed twenty-two people in Canada's deadliest mass shooting, Prime Minister Justin Trudeau announced a ban on "assault-style" firearms.. The legislation also required those who owned now-prohibited firearms to either participate in a buyback program or comply with a strict storage regime.

Australia

The inflection point for modern gun control in Australia was the Port Arthur massacre of 1996, when a young man killed thirty-five people and wounded nearly two dozen others. The rampage, perpetrated with a semiautomatic rifle, was the worst mass shooting in the nation's history. Less than two weeks later, the conservative-led national government pushed through fundamental changes to the country's gun laws in cooperation with the various states and territories, which regulate firearms.

The National Agreement on Firearms [PDF] all but prohibited automatic and semiautomatic assault rifles, mandated licensing and registration, and instituted a temporary gun buyback program that took some 650,000 assault weapons (about one-sixth of the national stock) out of public circulation. Among other things, the law also required licensees to demonstrate a "genuine need" for a particular type of gun and take a firearm safety course. After another high-profile shooting, in Melbourne in 2002, Australia's handgun laws were tightened as well. Many analysts said these measures were highly effective, citing declines in gun-death rates and gun-related mass killings.

Following an uptick in gun sales in 2017, however, Australian gun control advocates warned against the easing of gun laws in some states and territories. The gun safety discussion was also influenced by the suspected murder-suicide of a family of seven in Western Australia, the country's worst mass shooting in two decades. Today, Australia has more guns in circulation than before the Port Arthur massacre, although the number of people who own them has fallen over the same period.

Israel

Military service is compulsory in Israel, and guns are a part of many Israelis' daily lives. Much of the population has indirect access to an assault weapon by either being a soldier or a reservist or a relative of one. By law, most eighteen-year-olds are drafted into the military, psychologically screened, and provided at least some weapons training after high school. After serving typically two or three years in the armed forces, however, most Israelis are discharged and subject to civilian gun laws.

The country has relatively strict gun regulations, including an assault-weapons ban, a requirement to register ownership with the government, and a limit of one gun per owner. To obtain a gun license, an applicant must be an Israeli citizen or permanent resident; speak at least some Hebrew, Israel's official language; and pass a health screening. The minimum-age requirements vary: twenty-seven years old for citizens with no military or national-service experience, twenty-one for those who have served, and forty-five for permanent residents who are not citizens. Applicants must also show genuine cause to carry a firearm, such as self-defense or hunting.

United Kingdom

Modern gun control efforts in the United Kingdom (UK) have also been precipitated by extraordinary acts of violence that sparked public outrage. In 1987, a lone gunman armed with two semiautomatic rifles and a handgun went on a six-hour shooting spree roughly seventy miles west of London, killing more than a dozen people and then himself. In the wake of the incident, known as the Hungerford massacre, Britain introduced the Firearms (Amendment) Act, which expanded the list of banned weapons, including certain semiautomatic rifles, and increased registration requirements for other weapons.

A gun-related tragedy in the Scottish town of Dunblane in 1996 prompted Britain's strictest gun laws yet. A man armed with four handguns shot and killed sixteen schoolchildren and one adult before committing suicide in the country's worst mass shooting to date. The incident sparked a public campaign known as the Snowdrop Petition, which helped drive legislation banning handguns, with few exceptions. The government also instituted a temporary gun buyback program, which many credit with taking tens of thousands of illegal or unwanted guns out of supply.

A large majority of police officers in the UK do not carry firearms, setting them apart from counterparts in the United States and other countries. Guns are limited to specially trained police units that respond to particular emergencies or deploy for certain types of operations. Supporters of the policy say the unarmed officer symbolizes policing of the public by consent as opposed to by force.

Norway

Gun control had rarely been much of a political issue in Norway—where gun laws are viewed as tough, but ownership rates are high—until a right-wing extremist killed seventy-seven people in attacks in Oslo and at an island summer camp in 2011. Though Norway ranks fourteenth worldwide in gun ownership, according to Small Arms Survey, it placed near the bottom in gun homicide rates. (The U.S. rate is roughly forty-four times higher.) Most Norwegian police, like the British, do not carry firearms.

In the wake of the tragedy, some analysts in the United States cited the rampage as proof that strict gun laws—which in Norway include requiring applicants to be at least eighteen years of age, specify a "valid reason" for gun ownership, and obtain a government license—are ineffective. Other gun control critics have argued that had other Norwegians, including the police, been armed, the gunman might have been stopped earlier and killed fewer victims.

After the massacre, an independent commission recommended tightening Norway's gun restrictions in various ways, including by prohibiting pistols and semiautomatic weapons, but changes were not made. In 2018, the Norwegian parliament approved a ban on semiautomatic firearms, which took effect in 2021.

Japan

Gun control advocates regularly cite Japan's highly restrictive firearm regulations in tandem with its extraordinarily low gun death rate. Most years, fewer than one hundred Japanese die from gun violence in a country of 125 million people. Most guns are illegal in the country and ownership rates, which are quite low, reflect this.

Under Japan's firearm and sword law , the only guns permitted are shotguns, air guns, guns with specific research or industrial purposes, or those used for competitions. However, before access to these specialty weapons is granted, one must obtain formal instruction and pass a battery of written, mental, and drug tests and a rigorous background check. Furthermore, owners must inform the authorities of how their weapons and ammunition are stored and provide their firearms for annual inspection.

Some analysts link Japan's aversion to firearms with its demilitarization in the aftermath of World War II. Others say that because the overall crime rate in the country is so low, most Japanese see no need for firearms.

VIEWPOINT 5

> "The stricter gun laws of other 'advanced countries' have restrained homicidal violence, suicides and gun accidents—even when, in some cases, laws were introduced over massive protests from their armed citizens."

The United States Needs to Emulate Other Developed Nations in Gun Control

John Donohue

In the following viewpoint, John Donohue challenges the standard arguments offered by the gun lobby against any forms of gun control. Donohue analyzes how other countries are successfully controlling gun violence and asserts that the U.S. should follow their example. Many other developed countries understand that laws can help fight gun violence, according to this viewpoint. Donohue also explains how lax gun laws in the U.S. can endanger lives in other countries. John Donohue is an economist, lawyer, and professor of law at Stanford University.

As you read, consider the following questions:

1. Following the Newtown shooting of 2012, what percentage of Americans wanted background checks to be completed for gun purchases, as reported in this viewpoint?

"How US gun control compares to the rest of the world," by John Donohue, The Conversation, June 24, 2015. https://theconversation.com/how-us-gun-control-compares-to-the-rest-of-the-world-43590. Licensed under CC-BY-ND 4.0 International.

145

2. What does Donohue claim would have happened by now if the NRA's assertion that guns help prevent violence were true?
3. How have Germany, Finland, Italy, France, Japan, and the United Kingdom tried to reduce firearm violence, as reported by this author?

In June the Charleston killings renewed the sporadic debates over whether gun control might have prevented this terrible tragedy. Four months on, the massacre at Umpqua Community College in Roseburg, Oregon has left nine dead.

And once again, as after Charleston, President Obama has spoken openly about his frustration with the fact that "this kind of mass violence does not happen in other advanced countries."

On October 1st he put it this way:

> We know that other countries, in response to one mass shooting, have been able to craft laws that almost eliminate mass shootings. Friends of ours, allies of ours—Great Britain, Australia, countries like ours. So we know there are ways to prevent it.

So far, however, the U.S. has not come up with "ways to prevent it." The National Rifle Association (NRA), it seems, has so much power over politicians that even when 90% of Americans (including a majority of NRA members) wanted universal background checks to be adopted following the Newtown killings of 2012, no federal action ensued. Certainly, the type of comprehensive response that has been effective in other countries is unlike to emerge in the United States.

The NRA stranglehold on appropriate anti-crime measures is only part of the problem, though.

The gun culture's worship of the magical protective capacities of guns and their power to be wielded against perceived enemies—including the federal government—is a message that resonates with troubled individuals from the Santa Barbara killer, who was seeking vengeance on women who had failed to perceive his greatness, to the Charleston killer who echoed the Tea Party mantra of taking back our country.

I've been researching gun violence—and what can be done to prevent it—in the U.S. for 25 years. The fact is that if NRA claims about the efficacy of guns in reducing crime were true, the U.S. would have the lowest homicide rate among industrialized nations instead of the highest homicide rate (by a wide margin).

The U.S. is by far the world leader in the number of guns in civilian hands. The stricter gun laws of other "advanced countries" have restrained homicidal violence, suicides and gun accidents—even when, in some cases, laws were introduced over massive protests from their armed citizens.

The State of Gun Control in the U.S.

Eighteen states in the U.S. and a number of cities including Chicago, New York and San Francisco have tried to reduce the unlawful use of guns as well as gun accidents by adopting laws to keep guns safely stored when they are not in use. Safe storage is a common form of gun regulation in nations with stricter gun regulations.

The NRA has been battling such laws for years. But that effort was dealt a blow earlier this month when the U.S. Supreme Court—over a strident dissent by Justices Thomas and Scalia—refused to consider the San Francisco law that required guns not in use be stored safely. This was undoubtedly a positive step because hundreds of thousands of guns are stolen every year, and good public policy must try to keep guns out of the hands of criminals and children.

The dissenters, however, were alarmed by the thought that a gun stored in a safe would not be immediately available for use, but they seemed unaware of how unusual it is that a gun is helpful when someone is under attack.

For starters, only the tiniest fraction of victims of violent crime are able to use a gun in their defense. Over the period from 2007-2011, when roughly six million nonfatal violent crimes occurred each year, data from the National Crime Victimization Survey show that the victim did not defend with a gun in 99.2% of these incidents—this in a country with 300 million guns in civilian hands.

In fact, a study of 198 cases of unwanted entry into occupied single-family dwellings in Atlanta (not limited to night when the residents were sleeping) found that the invader was twice as likely to obtain the victim's gun than to have the victim use a firearm in self-defense.

The author of the study, Arthur Kellerman, concluded in words that Justice Thomas and Scalia might well heed: "On average, the gun that represents the greatest threat is the one that is kept loaded and readily available in a bedside drawer."

A loaded, unsecured gun in the home is like an insurance policy that fails to deliver at least 95% of the time you need it, but has the constant potential—particularly in the case of handguns that are more easily manipulated by children and more attractive for use in crime—to harm someone in the home or (via theft) the public at large.

More Guns Won't Stop Gun Violence

For years, the NRA mantra has been that allowing citizens to carry concealed handguns would reduce crime as they fought off or scared off the criminals.

Some early studies even purported to show that so-called right to carry laws (RTC) did just that, but a 2004 report from the National Research Council refuted that claim (saying it was not supported by "the scientific evidence"), while remaining uncertain about what the true impact of RTC laws was.

Ten years of additional data have allowed new research to get a better fix on this question, which is important since the NRA is pushing for a Supreme Court decision that would allow RTC as a matter of constitutional law.

The new research on this issue from my research team at Stanford University has given the most compelling evidence to date that RTC laws are associated with significant increases in violent crime—particularly for aggravated assault. Looking at Uniform

Crime Reports data from 1979-2012, we find that, on average, the 33 states that adopted RTC laws over this period experienced violent crime rates that are 4%-19% higher after 10 years than if they had not adopted these laws.

This hardly makes a strong case for RTC as a constitutional right. At the very least more research is needed to estimate more precisely exactly how much violent crime such a decision would unleash in the states that have so far resisted the NRA-backed RTC laws.

In the meantime, can anything make American politicians listen to the preferences of the 90% on the wisdom of adopting universal background checks for gun purchases?

Gun Control Around the World

As an academic exercise, one might speculate whether law could play a constructive role in reducing the number or deadliness of mass shootings.

Most other advanced nations apparently think so, since they make it far harder for someone like the Charleston killer to get his hands on a Glock semiautomatic handgun or any other kind of firearm (universal background checks are common features of gun regulation in other developed countries).

- Germany: To buy a gun, anyone under the age of 25 has to pass a psychiatric evaluation (presumably 21-year-old Dylann Roof would have failed).
- Finland: Handgun license applicants are only allowed to purchase firearms if they can prove they are active members of regulated shooting clubs. Before they can get a gun, applicants must pass an aptitude test, submit to a police interview, and show they have a proper gun storage unit.
- Italy: To secure a gun permit, one must establish a genuine reason to possess a firearm and pass a background check considering both criminal and mental health records (again, presumably Dylann Roof would have failed).

- France: Firearms applicants must have no criminal record and pass a background check that considers the reason for the gun purchase and evaluates the criminal, mental, and health records of the applicant. (Dylann Roof would presumably have failed in this process).
- United Kingdom and Japan: Handguns are illegal for private citizens.

While mass shootings as well as gun homicides and suicides are not unknown in these countries, the overall rates are substantially higher in the United States than in these competitor nations.

While NRA supporters frequently challenge me on these statistics saying that this is only because "American blacks are so violent," it is important to note that white murder rates in the U.S. are well over twice as high as the murder rates in any of these other countries.

Australia Hasn't Had a Mass Shooting Since 1996

The story of Australia, which had 13 mass shootings in the 18-year period from 1979 to 1996 but none in the succeeding 19 years, is worth examining.

The turning point was the 1996 Port Arthur massacre in Tasmania, in which a gunman killed 35 individuals using semiautomatic weapons.

In the wake of the massacre, the conservative federal government succeeded in implementing tough new gun control laws throughout the country. A large array of weapons were banned—including the Glock semiautomatic handgun used in the Charleston shootings. The government also imposed a mandatory gun buyback that substantially reduced gun possession in Australia.

The effect was that both gun suicides and homicides (as well as total suicides and homicides) fell. In addition, the 1996 legislation made it a crime to use firearms in self-defense.

When I mention this to disbelieving NRA supporters they insist that crime must now be rampant in Australia. In fact, the Australian murder rate has fallen to close one per 100,000 while the

U.S. rate, thankfully lower than in the early 1990s, is still roughly at 4.5 per 100,000—over four times as high. Moreover, robberies in Australia occur at only about half the rate of the U.S. (58 in Australia versus 113.1 per 100,000 in the US in 2012).

How did Australia do it? Politically, it took a brave prime minister to face the rage of Australian gun interests.

John Howard wore a bullet-proof vest when he announced the proposed gun restrictions in June 1996. The deputy prime minister was hung in effigy. But Australia did not have a domestic gun industry to oppose the new measures so the will of the people was allowed to emerge. And today, support for the safer, gun-restricted Australia is so strong that going back would not be tolerated by the public.

That Australia hasn't had a mass shooting since 1996 is likely more than merely the result of the considerable reduction in guns—it's certainly not the case that guns have disappeared altogether.

I suspect that the country has also experienced a cultural shift between the shock of the Port Arthur massacre and the removal of guns from every day life as they are no longer available for self-defense and they are simply less present throughout the country. Troubled individuals, in other words, are not constantly being reminded that guns are a means to address their alleged grievances to the extent that they were in the past, or continue to be in the U.S.

Lax Gun Control in One Country Can Create Problems in Another

Of course, strict gun regulations cannot ensure that the danger of mass shootings or killings has been eliminated.

Norway has strong gun control and committed humane values. But they didn't prevent Anders Breivik from opening fire on a youth camp on the island of Utoya in 2011? His clean criminal record and hunting license had allowed him to secure semiautomatic rifles, but Norway restricted his ability to get high-capacity clips for them. In his manifesto, Breivik wrote about his attempts to legally buy weapons, stating, "I envy our European American brothers as the gun laws in Europe sucks ass in comparison."

In fact, in the same manifesto ("December and January – Rifle/gun accessories purchased") Breivik wrote that it was from a U.S. supplier that he purchased—and had mailed—ten 30-round ammunition magazines for the rifle he used in his attack.

In other words, even if a particular state chooses to make it harder for some would-be killers to get their weapons, these efforts can be undercut by the jurisdictions that hold out from these efforts. In the U.S., of course, gun control measures at the state and local level are often thwarted by the lax attitude to gun acquisition in other states.

VIEWPOINT 6

> "'The federal government has a history of starting research programs to address big safety or public health problems such as smoking, HIV/AIDS, and traffic accidents,' he notes. 'We haven't had anything like that for firearms violence.'"

Federal Funding for Firearms Research Must Expand to Stem Gun Violence

Kirsten Weir

In the following viewpoint, Kirsten Weir advocates for more research backed by the federal government as a tool to stem gun violence and death. Weir provides statistics on how the federal government provides research funding for other public health issues such as smoking or traffic accidents. She argues that much about gun violence is not well understood because of the lack of federally funded research. Weir points to some funding beginning to take root but maintains that efforts must be greatly expanded. Kirsten Weir is a freelance writer focusing on conservation, psychology, science, and health.

As you read, consider the following questions:

1. As reported by Weir, how many firearm deaths occur each year in the U.S.?

"A thaw in the freeze on federal funding for gun violence and injury prevention research," by Kirsten Weir, American Psychological Association, April 1, 2021. Reprinted by permission.

2. How can the program ShootSafe impact gun violence, according to this viewpoint?
3. Which organization has partnered with medical and public health groups to bolster research funding, according to this viewpoint?

Mass shootings are among the most high-profile examples of gun violence in the United States. But every day, firearms take a quiet toll in towns and cities across the country in the form of violent criminal activity, intimate partner violence, accidental injury, and suicide. Approximately 40,000 U.S. deaths—about 109 per day—are caused by firearms each year, according to Centers for Disease Control and Prevention (CDC) statistics.

Despite that deadly tally, there has been no dedicated federal funding for gun violence and injury prevention for more than two decades—until now. In fiscal year 2020, the Labor, Health and Human Services, Education, and Related Agencies appropriations bill included $25 million for gun violence research, split evenly between the CDC and the National Institutes of Health (NIH). The NIH grants were distributed by a variety of institutes, including the National Institute of Mental Health (NIMH). Among the recipients of the CDC and NIH funding are many psychologists who hope to better understand, and ultimately prevent, deaths and injuries due to firearms.

"When this many of our neighbors and family are dying by firearms, it merits attention. But the field has been neglected," says Andrew Morral, PhD, a senior behavioral scientist at RAND Corporation and director of the National Collaborative on Gun Violence Research. He received a CDC grant in September 2020 to study household firearms ownership and is hopeful this new dedicated funding may be a turning point. "The federal government has a history of starting research programs to address big safety or public health problems such as smoking, HIV/AIDS, and traffic accidents," he notes. "We haven't had anything like that for firearms violence, but I think this could be the start of a real flourishing."

A History of the Funding Freeze

In 1993, Arthur Kellermann, MD, then at the University of Tennessee, and colleagues published a highly publicized paper that found keeping a gun in the home was strongly associated with an increased risk of homicide by an intimate acquaintance or family member (*The New England Journal of Medicine*, Vol. 329, No. 15, 1993). After the paper's publication, the National Rifle Association lobbied for the elimination of the CDC's National Center for Injury Prevention and Control, which funded the study. In 1996, Congress responded by passing an appropriations bill that stated that "none of the funds made available for injury prevention and control at the Centers for Disease Control and Prevention may be used to advocate or promote gun control." In the 1997 budget, the $2.6 million that the CDC had invested in firearms research the previous year was shifted to research on traumatic brain injuries.

The amendment to the appropriations bill didn't explicitly ban research on gun violence. But its vague wording made it hard for the federal research agencies to know what was and wasn't allowed. Equivalent language was later added to the legislation that funded the NIH. In both the NIH and CDC, funding for gun violence and injury research ground to a halt—a chilling effect that lasted for two decades. After mounting public pressure to address gun violence, however, congressional leaders clarified in 2018 that the rule applies specifically to gun control advocacy and does not prevent the CDC from funding gun violence research. That clarification opened the door for research awards in 2020.

While some researchers have continued to do work on firearms violence with funding from private foundations or state grants, the lack of federal funding has set the field back, Morral says. An analysis by David E. Stark, MD, and Nigam H. Shah, MBBS, PhD, found that gun violence was associated with significantly less funding and fewer publications than public health problems of a similar scale. While gun violence and sepsis kill about the same number of people each year, funding for gun violence research from 2004 to 2015 was just 0.7% of that for sepsis, and the publication volume was just 4% of that for sepsis. Gun violence was the least researched of the 30 leading causes of death, and the second-least funded after falls (*JAMA*, Vol. 317, No. 1, 2017).

"Private foundations have been keeping the lights on. But this new federal funding is a big deal for the field," Morral says.

New Research Underway

Given the dearth of research funding, there are big gaps in our basic understanding of gun ownership and gun violence. "Without a doubt, we're way behind in this area of injury prevention research. In the field of suicide prevention, the lack of federal funding has hamstrung us for decades," says Craig Bryan, PsyD, ABPP, director of the Division of Recovery and Resilience at The Ohio State University College of Medicine. "The majority of suicide deaths in the U.S. involve a firearm, yet we know very little."

Bryan was awarded an NIMH grant to study the mechanisms underlying the association of firearms availability and vulnerability to suicide. He and his colleagues are recruiting both non-gun owners and gun owners, including those who regularly carry a firearm and those who do not. Some of the participants report having been suicidal in the past. The exploratory study will involve interviews, self-report surveys, and behavioral tasks to investigate how participants respond to predictable and unpredictable threats. "The central idea is to study the psychological processes that contribute to people wanting to acquire a firearm," Bryan says. "We hope this will help us identify where to focus our future efforts so we're not just stabbing in the dark."

Many open questions remain about the psychology of gun ownership. But there's also a lack of understanding about who owns guns in the first place. Morral is the lead investigator on a CDC-funded project that aims to develop gun ownership estimates for various strata of the population, including groups defined by race, age, gender, marital status, and urban versus rural location. Without such basic data about who owns guns, he says, it's impossible to identify which policy interventions might be most effective for reducing gun violence and injury in specific populations. "Firearms violence and suicide is very disproportionately distributed across different groups," he says. "We hope to use these estimates to do more sensitive analyses of the effects of different gun policies."

While the funding freeze hampered basic knowledge on gun violence, it also blocked the pipeline of new researchers entering the field. Krista Mehari, PhD, an assistant professor of psychology at the University of South Alabama, entered graduate school with a plan to study gun violence, but given the challenge of securing funding, her adviser steered her toward studying violence more broadly. As a postdoctoral fellow, she tried again to focus on guns—and again, faculty urged her toward topics with more available grants. "I was delighted when the CDC announced awards in gun injury prevention," she says. "It felt like an opportunity to finally do the work I've wanted to do for a long time."

Mehari now has CDC funding to study risky gun-related behaviors and the acceptability of prevention approaches among Black boys and young men (the population at the greatest risk of death by homicide with a firearm, according to research) and among older White men (those who studies show are most at risk of suicide). She and her colleagues will begin with qualitative research to understand attitudes and practices around gun use and violence prevention strategies, which they'll use to develop a national survey. In both homicide and suicide prevention, there has often been a focus on taking away guns, Mehari says. "The problem is, there's a cultural disconnect between the people who own and use guns and those who are working to prevent deaths completed with the use of guns. That leads to prevention strategies that aren't ecologically valid," she says. "The goal of our project is to try to start bridging that gap."

Gun control remains a hot-button political issue, and other researchers are also seeking common ground between gun ownership and safety. David Schwebel, PhD, a professor at the University of Alabama at Birmingham, and colleagues have a CDC grant to develop and evaluate an interactive website, called ShootSafe, designed to teach children how to engage safely with firearms to reduce the risk of accidental injuries and deaths from guns. "We know children in our country are using firearms for hunting and shooting recreationally, and it's not realistic to stop that from happening. So how can we use psychological science to reduce tragic accidents?" says Schwebel, whose background is in pediatric injury prevention. "As psychologists, we already know a good deal about how to change behavior. We're taking what we've learned from things like dog bite prevention or poisoning prevention and applying it to the issue of unintentional firearms injuries."

This type of research would have been impossible a few years ago, he adds. "We could never have done a project of this size and scope without federal funding."

APA Advocacy Efforts

Restoring funding for firearms research didn't come easily. For years, organizations including APA have been engaged in advocacy efforts to support funding for gun violence prevention. The APA Resolution on Firearm Violence Research and Prevention, approved by APA's Council of Representatives in 2014, calls for a science-based public health approach to gun violence research and prevention. In 2018, APA and more than a dozen medical and public health groups partnered with Giffords, the gun violence prevention organization founded by former U.S. Rep. Gabrielle Giffords, who survived a gunshot to the head in an assassination attempt in 2011. The 2018 partnership was forged in an effort to urge Congress to fund research to address gun violence. In 2019, APA CEO Arthur C. Evans Jr., PhD, spoke at a congressional roundtable event about the need for dedicated federal funding for gun violence prevention research.

While those efforts have begun to pay off, APA will continue to take an active role in advocating for support of gun violence research, says Ben Vonachen, senior director of congressional and federal relations at APA. "The $25 million of federal funding is a good down payment in terms of the need, but it gets our foot in the door," he says. "Through our advocacy efforts with other partners, we're hoping to build momentum to increase that amount over time."

Meanwhile, experts say that psychology has much to offer this public health crisis. "With every mass shooting, there is a growing consensus that we need to do something about this problem," Morral says. "Research is one of those things, and there is a real need for the methodological expertise of the kind that psychologists bring to the table."

The opportunities for psychological research are wide-ranging, says Mehari. "In many areas of psychology, things have been so heavily researched that to ask a novel question, you need an intensive study design and a lot of resources. Because of the slower momentum in the field of gun violence prevention, there is so much space to ask and answer a lot of important questions," she says.

The problem, she adds, is urgent. "We're losing so many people to gun violence, unnecessarily. And there is so much we don't know."

Periodical and Internet Sources Bibliography

The following articles have been selected to supplement the diverse views presented in this chapter.

Hilary Brueck, "Switzerland Has a Stunningly High Rate of Gun Ownership—Here's Why it Doesn't Have Mass Shootings," *Insider*, June 9, 2023. https://www.businessinsider.com/switzerland-gun-laws-rates-of-gun-deaths-2018-2.

Geovanna Coi, "Global Gun Violence and Laws Compared—By the Numbers," *Politico*, May 25, 2022. https://www.politico.eu/article/global-gun-violence-and-laws-compared-by-the-numbers/#:~:text=In%20the%20EU%20and%20in,have%20very%20relaxed%20gun%20laws.

Ashleigh DeLuca, "Understanding American Gun Violence Part 2: How to Solve the American Gun Epidemic," Temple University, December 7, 2022. https://news.temple.edu/news/2022-12-07/how-to-solve-American-gun-epidemic.

Miranda Dixon Luinenburg, "How to Prevent Gun Deaths Without Gun Control," Vox, June 3, 2022. https://www.vox.com/future-perfect/23150764/gun-violence-prevention-gun-control-jennifer-doleac.

Sean Gregory, "6 Real Ways We Can Reduce Gun Violence in America," *TIME*, March 22, 2018. https://time.com/5209901/gun-violence-america-reduction/.

Clay S. Jenkinson, "A European's Perspective on Gun Violence in America," Governing, July 17, 2022. https://www.governing.com/context/a-europeans-perspective-on-gun-violence-in-america.

Lisa Milbrand, "How to Help with Gun Control: 12 Things You Can Do Now to Stop Gun Violence," *Reader's Digest*, March 27, 2023. https://www.rd.com/article/how-to-help-with-gun-control/.

Sallyann Nicholls, "How Does Europe Compare with the US on Gun Ownership?" Euronews, June 8, 2019. https://www.euronews.com/2019/08/05/which-european-country-boasts-the-most-guns-.

Rachel Treisman, "One Way to Prevent Gun Violence? Treat It as a Public Health Issue," NPR, May 12, 2023. https://www.npr.org/2023/05/12/1173141518/gun-violence-prevention-public-health.

For Further Discussion

Chapter 1
1. Does the Constitution's Second Amendment support gun ownership as it is defined in modern society? Use information from the viewpoints in this chapter to support your response.
2. Using the statistics presented in this chapter, what impact does the availability of guns have on children and teens? What could be done to alleviate this problem?
3. Based on the information you've read in these viewpoints, does it seem likely that the United States could institute gun control policies like those used in Australia and New Zealand? Why or why not?

Chapter 2
1. Do American citizens have an effect on gun control? Back up your argument with specific details from the viewpoints in this chapter.
2. How does the NRA impact gun control legislation, based on what you've read in this chapter?
3. What are some of the arguments in this chapter in support of arming teachers? What are some of the arguments against arming teachers?

Chapter 3
1. What is the connection between gunmakers, the gun lobby, money, and political contributions? Support your answer with evidence from two different viewpoints in this chapter.
2. Should gun makers be held legally liable when one of their products is used to kill someone? Why or why not?
3. What are some of the psychological and social impacts of gun violence mentioned in the viewpoint by Arash Javanbakht?

For Further Discussion

Chapter 4

1. What is the Great Replacement Theory and how does it motivate gun violence extremists, according to the viewpoint by Michael Lyle?
2. What laws and policies in other countries are cited as examples of successful gun control? Do you think these laws could be passed in the U.S.? Why or why not?
3. Do you think firearm safety programs like ShootSafe could help effectively curb gun-related injuries and deaths? Explain your answer.

Organizations to Contact

The editors have compiled the following list of organizations concerned with the issues debated in this book. The descriptions are derived from materials provided by the organizations. All have publications or information available for interested readers. The list was compiled on the date of publication of the present volume; the information provided here may change. Be aware that many organizations take several weeks or longer to respond to inquiries, so allow as much time as possible.

American Psychological Association (APA)
750 First Street, NE
Washington, DC 20002
(800) 374-2721
website: www.apa.org

The American Psychological Association sees its mission as one of advancing psychology to benefit society and improve lives. Its website includes information about gun violence and crime along with podcasts, advocacy groups, readings, and a variety of publications.

Brady
840 First Street, NE
Suite 400
Washington, DC 20002
(202) 370-8100
website: www.bradyunited.org

Brady is a gun violence prevention organization that attacks this complex problem from all angles. It is named after Jim Brady, a Republican, gun owner, and press secretary to former President Ronald Reagan. Brady also survived a gunshot wound to the head. The organization seeks to prevent every community from the daily toll of mass shootings and gun violence from a bipartisan perspective.

Centers for Disease Control and Prevention (CDC)

1600 Clifton Road
Atlanta, GA 30329
(800) 232-4636
website: www.cdc.gov

The Centers for Disease Control and Prevention is the national public health agency of the United States. It is dedicated to protecting the health and well-being of U.S. citizens, which includes researching and advising on gun violence.

Everytown for Gun Safety

PO Box 3886
New York, NY 10163
(646) 324-8250
website: www.everytown.org

Everytown is an American non-profit gun violence prevention organization. This organization's website demonstrates how everyday Americans are helping win the fight for gun safety and offers statistics on gun violence.

Giffords

268 Bush Street #555
San Francisco, CA 94104
(415) 433-2062
email: info@giffords.org
website: https://giffords.org/

Giffords is an organization was started by former Arizona Congresswoman Gabrielle Giffords who survived a gun violence incident. It aims to help lead the fight for gun safety.

March for Our Lives

PO Box 3417
New York, NY 10008
website: https://marchforourlives.com/

March for Our Lives is a student-led group dedicated to guiding young people in taking action against and stopping gun violence. It supports collective action, including signing petitions and organizing demonstrations.

Moms Demand Action

website: https://momsdemandaction.org/

Moms Demand Action is a grassroots movement of Americans fighting for public safety measures that can help protect people from gun violence. This organization has groups in every U.S. state.

National Collaborative on Gun Violence Research

1776 Main Street
Santa Monica, CA 90401
(301) 496-4000
website: www.ncgvr.org

The National Collaborative on Gun Violence Research seeks to back scientific research on the topic of gun violence and then use this information to provide citizens and policymakers with the facts to combat gun violence. It aims to fund and disseminate research supporting effective gun policies.

National Institutes of Health (NIH)

9000 Rockville Pike
Bethesda, MD 20892
(301) 496-4000
website: www.nih.gov

The National Institutes of Health is a U.S. governmental agency with an interest in protecting all Americans through providing timely information about public health threats, including that of gun violence. It funds research on public health-related issues.

Sandy Hook Promise

PO Box 3489
Newtown, CT 06470
(203) 304-9780
website: www.sandyhookpromise.org

Sandy Hook Promise is a non-profit organization that was founded and led by the families of those who were killed in the Sandy Hook mass shooting in 2012. Its mission is to educate and empower youth and adults to prevent violence in communities, homes, and schools.

Bibliography of Books

John Allen. *Thinking Critically: Gun Control*. San Diego, CA: Reference Point Press, 2018.

Laurie Collier Hillstrom. *School Shootings and the Never Again Movement*. Santa Barbara, CA: ABC-CLIO, 2019.

Matt Doeden. *Gun Violence: Fighting for Our Lives and Our Rights*. Minneapolis, MN: Twenty-First Century Books, 2020.

Ellen Hopkins. *People Kill People*. New York, NY: Margaret K. McElderry, 2018.

Tim Mak. *Misfire: Inside the Downfall of the NRA*. New York, NY: Dutton, 2021.

Kyrie McCauley. *We Can Be Heroes*. New York, NY: Katherine Tegen Books, 2021.

Carla Mooney. *How Can Gun Violence Be Stopped?* San Diego, CA: Reference Point Press, 2021.

Kindra Neely. *Numb to This: A Memoir of a Mass Shooting*. New York, NY: Little Brown & Company, 2022.

Jean Rawitt. *Inspired to Action: How Young Changemakers Can Shape their Communities and the World*. Lanham, MD: Rowman & Littlefield, 2023.

Jason Reynolds. *Long Way Down*. New York, NY: Atheneum, 2017.

Barbara Sheen. *Teen Activists: Youth Changing the World*. San Diego, CA: Reference Point Press, 2023.

Bradley Steffens. *Gun Violence and Mass Shootings*. San Diego, CA: Reference Point Press, 2019.

Todd Strasser. *Give a Boy a Gun*. New York, NY: Simon & Schuster, 2020.

Elizabeth Williamson. *Sandy Hook: An American Tragedy and the Battle for Truth*. New York, NY: Dutton, 2022.

Index

A

Abbott, Greg, 35, 90
American Legislative Exchange Council, 96
American Psychological Association, 158–159
American Revolution, 20, 48
ammunition, 39
anti-government extremism, 127–129
Ardern, Jacinda, 39–41
Associated Press-NORC Center for Public Affairs Research, 121–125
Australian Bureau of Statistics, 99, 101
Australian Institute of Criminology, 40
Australian Institute of Health and Welfare, 99
automatic handguns, 14

B

Barnhart, Michelle, 62–66
Battle Born Progress, 128–129
Beasley, Ashbey, 31–33
Bellesiles, Michael, 47
Biden, Joe, 35, 47, 52, 55, 57, 59, 68, 78, 80, 89, 127
Bloomberg, Mike, 92
Blunt, Roy, 55

Brady Center to Prevent Gun Violence, 105
Breivik, Anders, 151–152
Bright, David, 97–103
Brodeur, Abel, 112–113
Bryan, Craig, 156
Build Back Better plan, 55
Bundy, Cliven, 128
Bureau of Land Management (U.S.), 128
Burr, Richard, 55

C

Carter, Patrick, 25–29
Center for American Progress, 127
Center for Violence Prevention (University of Texas), 23
Centers for Disease Control and Prevention, 23, 31–33, 61, 154–158
Chaplin, Danny, 49
children/teens, 25–33, 138
Clinton, Bill, 22
Clinton, Hillary, 22, 24
Colonial America, 20, 46
Congress (U.S.), 22–23, 28, 37, 51–55, 57–60, 74–76, 78–80, 82, 88–92, 104–105, 127–129, 138–139, 155, 158
Cook, Philip, 33
Cornyn, John, 52–54
crisis intervention, 23

Index

Cruz, Ted, 35, 90, 92
Cunningham, Rebecca, 25–29

D

defund police, 48
Dickey, Jay, 28
Dick's Sporting Goods, 108
divestment, 108
Donohue, John, 145–152
Duke University, 33

E

economy, 86–117
Edmund, Marissa, 127–128
election, 54–55, 58, 60, 74, 87, 89–92, 128
Evans, Arthur C., Jr., 158
Everytown for Gun Safety, 32, 92

F

federal research, 153–159
Firearm Safety Among Children and Teens Consortium, 28–29
firearm training, 64
Firearms Amendment Act (U.K.), 142
Firearms Control Act (South Africa), 131–134
Fischer, Tim, 98–99, 101–102
Frois, Luis, 49

G

gender, 68, 157
Giffords, Gabby, 90, 158

Giffords organization, 90, 92, 129, 158
Gift, Thomas, 56–61
gun availability, 20, 24, 27, 79
gun buyback, 39–40, 87, 97–103, 141, 150
gun collecting, 18
gun control policies, 45
  Australia, 18, 38–41, 48, 97–101, 141–142, 146, 150–151
  Canada, 140
  Finland, 149
  France, 150
  Germany, 149
  Israel, 142
  Italy, 149
  Japan, 46, 48–49, 144, 150
  Mozambique, 134
  New Zealand, 18, 38–41
  Norway, 143–144, 151
  South Africa, 130–136
  United Kingdom, 142–143, 146, 150
  United States, *See* laws (U.S.) *and* Second Amendment
Gun Free South Africa, 131
gun ownership, 20–21, 28, 35–36, 41, 45, 47–48, 68–70, 79, 82–83, 156–158
gun storage, 28–29, 133, 135, 147–148
gun use on job, 18
Gun Violence Archive, 61

171

H

Hammer, Marion, 96
Harvard University, 32, 75
Hemenway, David, 32–33
Hideyoshi, Toyotomi, 48–49
Howard, John, 38–39, 98–100, 151
Huff, Aimee Dinnin, 62–66
hunting, 18, 21, 28, 95–96

I

Institute for a Progressive Nevada, 127
Institute for Firearm Injury Prevention (University of Michigan), 33

J

January 6 Capitol riots, 128
Javanbakht, Arash, 110–116
Johns Hopkins Center for Gun Violence Solutions, 31–32
Jones, David R., 51–55

K

Kellerman, Arthur, 148, 155
Kennedy, John, 91

L

Lamb, Guy, 130–136
LaPierre, Wayne, 24
laws (U.S.), 75
   age-based laws, 53, 139
   arming teachers, 18, 45, 57, 62–66, 71–72
   assault weapons ban, 22, 47, 55, 58, 71, 74, 127, 129, 139
   background checks, 22, 24, 36–37, 47–48, 53, 55, 58, 68, 74, 129, 139, 146, 149
   Bipartisan Safer Communities Act, 52, 78–82, 127
   boyfriend loophole, 53, 59, 127, 135
   Brady Handgun Violence Prevention Act, 139
   concealed carry, 18, 24, 71, 139
   Gun Control Act of 1968, 139
   high-capacity ammunition ban, 58, 71, 127, 129, 139–140
   mental illness, 22–23, 53, 57, 123, 135, 139
   national database, 22, 24
   Protection of Lawful Commerce in Arms Act, 105
   red flag law, 53, 59, 127, 135
   registry/database, 48, 71
   right to carry, 148–149
   school safety measures, 53, 57, 63–66
   stand your ground, 96
   waiting period, 53, 127
Laxalt, Adam, 128
Lee, Susie, 129
Lee, Wang-Sheng, 99
Leigh, Andrew, 99
lobbyists, 15, 18, 35, 45, 58, 87–92, 96, 107–108
Loeffler, Kelly, 92

Index

Ludwig, Jens, 122
Lyle, Michael, 126–129

M

Magnus, Annette, 128
manufacturers, 15, 96, 104–109
  Anderson Manufacturing, 94
  Daniel Defense, 87
  Glock, 94, 149–150
  Kimber Manufacturing, 94
  Remington Arms, 94, 107–108
  Savage Arms, 94
  SCCY Industries, 94
  Sig Sauer, 94
  Smith & Wesson, 87, 94–95, 107
  Sturm, Ruger & Co, 87, 94, 108
  Winchester, 14
Martin, Trayvon, 96
mass shooting, 18, 36, 45, 50, 61, 70, 75, 79, 90, 94, 102–103, 105, 110–116, 123, 154, 159
  Atlanta spas, 47, 74
  Boulder, Colorado, supermarket, 47, 74
  Buffalo, New York, supermarket, 35, 51–55, 59, 128
  Charleston, South Carolina, church, 74, 146–147, 149–150
  Christchurch, New Zealand, mosque, 39
  Columbine High School, 60, 64, 66
  Dunblane, Scotland, school, 143
  El Paso, Texas, Walmart, 74
  Highland Park, Illinois, parade, 31, 78
  Highlands Ranch, Colorado, school, 111
  Hungerford massacre, U.K., 142
  Isla Vista, California, killings, 146–147
  Las Vegas concert, 74, 98, 106, 139
  Monash University, Australia, 141
  Montreal, Canada, school, 140
  Nashville, Tennessee, school, 31–32
  Nova Scotia, Canada, spree, 141
  Orlando, Florida, nightclub, 20, 22, 24, 74, 106
  Oslo, Norway, summer camp, 143–144, 151–152
  Osmington, Australia, family, 141
  Parkland, Florida, school, 60, 64, 66, 74, 76, 106–107, 139
  Port Arthur, Australia, 39–41, 98, 100–101, 141–142, 150–151
  Quebec City, Canada, mosque, 140
  Roseburg, Oregon, college, 74, 146
  San Bernardino, California, workplace, 74, 76
  San Diego, California, synagogue, 111
  Sandy Hook school, 24, 27, 60, 74, 76, 89, 92, 106–108, 146
  Tree of Life synagogue, 115

Tucson, Arizona, supermarket, 74, 158. *See also* Giffords, Gabby
University of North Carolina at Charlotte, 111
Uvalde, Texas, school, 31, 35, 51–55, 57, 60, 63–64, 89, 127–128, 138
Masters, Jonathan, 137–144
McConaughey, Matthew, 53
McConnell, Mitch, 54
McDermott, Monika L., 51–55
McSally, Martha, 92
Mehari, Krista, 157, 159
Melham, Diana, 98–101
mental health, 22–23, 27, 53, 57, 94, 110–116, 134–135, 154
Morral, Andrew, 154–157, 159
Murkowski, Lisa, 54–55
Murphy, Chris, 37, 52, 55, 59, 92

N

National Collaborative on Gun Violence Research, 154
National Crime Victimization Survey, 147–148
National Education Association, 63
National Firearms Agreement (Australia), 39–41, 99–103, 141
National Instant Criminal Background Check System (FBI), 68
National Institute of Mental Health, 154, 156
National Institutes of Health, 28, 154–155
National Research Council, 148
National Rifle Association, 14, 18, 24, 35–37, 45, 47, 50, 56–61, 87, 90–91, 96, 107–108, 146–150, 155
National Shooting Sports Foundation, 106
Neill, Christine, 99

O

Oath Keepers, 128
Obama, Barack, 48, 54, 89, 106–107, 146
Ohio State University College of Medicine, 156
OpenSecrets, 91–92

P

Parker, Jonathan, 19–24
partisanship, 18, 24, 34–37, 60
  Democrats, 15, 45, 47, 51–55, 57–59, 68–72, 74–76, 78–83, 89, 127, 129
  independents, 15, 68, 78
  Republicans, 15, 22, 36, 45, 51–55, 57–59, 63–64, 68–72, 74–83, 89–91
  Tea Party, 147
Paul, Rand, 91
Pear, Veronica, 32
Perdue, David, 92
personal protection/self-defense, 15, 18, 21–22, 48, 66, 69, 95–96, 123, 131, 142, 147–148, 150
Pew Research Center, 15, 18, 28, 67–69, 77–83

Poliquin, Christopher, 73–76
PolitiFact, 30–33
Portman, Rob, 55
protest/rally
  anti-gun, 18, 31, 76
  pro-gun, 18, 107
Proud Boys, 128

R

race/ethnicity, 27, 47, 65, 69, 80, 122, 156–157. *See also* white supremacy
RAND Corporation, 154
Roof, Dylann, 149–150
Roston, Allen, 104–109
rural communities, 27, 29, 68–69, 71–72, 123, 157

S

Sandy Hook Promise, 92
Sarat, Austin, 34–37
Sarre, Rick, 38–41
Scalia, Antonin, 147–148
Scalise, Steve, 91
Schaeffer, Katherine, 67–72
Schiff, Adam, 89
school shooting, 24, 27, 29, 31–32, 35–36, 51–55, 57, 60, 63–66, 89, 94
Schumer, Chuck, 31, 55
Schwebel, David, 158
Second Amendment, 15, 18–24, 35–37, 50, 52, 57, 68, 90, 120, 138–139
Shah, Nigam H., 155

Sherman, Amy, 30–33
ShootSafe, 158
Siegel, Michael, 93–96
Snowdrop Petition, 143
Sporting Shooters Association of Australia NSW, 98–99
sport shooting, 18, 29, 95–96
Stanford University, 148
Stark, David E., 155
Stepansky, Joseph, 88–92
Stepman, Jarrett, 46–50
Suardi, Sandy, 99
substance abuse, 23
suicide, 23, 29, 101–103, 134, 141, 150, 154, 156–157
Supreme Court (U.S.), 20, 139, 147–148
  Citizens United v. FEC, 91
  District of Columbia v. Heller, 21
  McDonald v. Chicago, 21

T

target practice, 28
Temple, Jeff, 23
Thomas, Clarence, 147–148
Toomey, Pat, 55
Trudeau, Justin, 141
Trump, Donald, 24, 35, 57, 90–91, 128
Tsai, Brian, 33
Turnbull, Malcolm, 98

U

Uniform Crime Reports, 148–149

United Nations, 132
University of Alabama at Birmingham, 158
University of California, Los Angeles, 75
University of Chicago Harris School of Public Policy, 121–125
University of South Alabama, 157
urban communities, 27, 68–69, 71–72, 122–123, 157

V

Violence Prevention Research Program (University of California, Davis), 32
Vonachen, Ben, 159

W

Washington, George, 49
Weir, Kirsten, 153–159
white supremacy, 127–128
Wits University School of Governance, 132

Y

Young, Tod, 55
Yousaf, Hasin, 112–113

Z

Zimmerman, George, 96
Zimmerman, Marc A., 25–29